# LIFELIKE ANIMALS

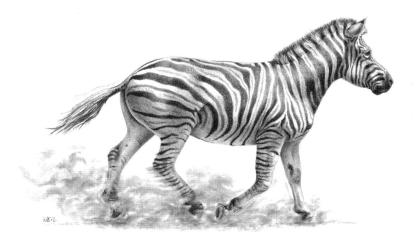

## By Linda Weil

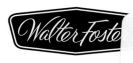

www.walterfoster.com

D1377438

7  9  10  8

# CONTENTS

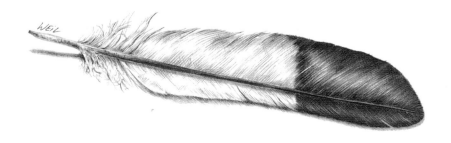

# INTRODUCTION

Drawing is my first love, and pencil is my favorite medium. Although I have worked with many different media, I always return to graphite pencil with joy. The natural world is my preferred field, especially wild animals. In a successful drawing, the personality of the animal will shine through to make a statement about the animal's place in the world, its specific environment, and its relationship to others. Every animal is unique, and I try to show this in my drawings.

In this book, I'll share with you the various techniques and methods I use to create finished artwork in graphite pencil. Other artists may use different methods and techniques to achieve similar results. You should explore many different ways of drawing until you find those you are comfortable with and that suit your personal style.

There are two secrets to a successful drawing. The first is to have fun doing it, as your enjoyment will show in your work. The second is practice—the more you draw, the more confident you will become, and the more accurate your drawings will be. Take a sketchbook with you wherever you go, and try to draw something every day. Keep all your drawings—even those you don't feel are successful—because they are important records of your progress. Remember, every drawing is a learning experience, and not every drawing needs to be a masterpiece!

I hope you enjoy reading and using this book as much as I have enjoyed writing it for you. Happy drawing!

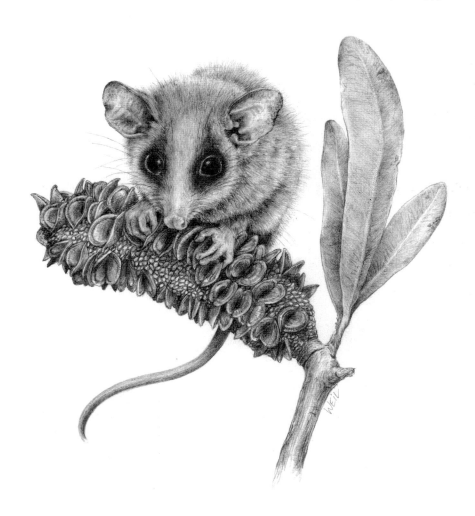

# TOOLS AND MATERIALS

With just a piece of paper and a pencil, you can draw almost anywhere, anytime. Although there is an ever-increasing range of materials available to you, it's best to start with only the basics; you can expand your collection as your skills develop. Here you'll find information about some basic materials that are good for beginners. Try to purchase the highest-quality materials your budget will allow, as these provide the best results. There is nothing more frustrating than being limited by scratchy pencils or paper that tears!

▶ **Pencils** Soft pencils (labeled "B") produce strong, black tones; hard pencils (labeled "H") create lighter marks. The higher the number that accompanies the letter, the harder or softer the lead. (For example, a 4B pencil is softer than a 2B pencil.) HB and F pencils are used for middle grades. I recommend starting with the following range of wood-cased pencils: 2H, H, HB, F, B, and 2B. As your skills develop, you can experiment with different types of pencils. I like to use a clutch pencil for the 2H, HB, and 2B grades—this is similar to a mechanical pencil, but it holds a thicker 2 mm lead, which is ideal for broad strokes. You also can purchase woodless graphite pencils, which are great for covering large areas with tone or for making quick sketches. These pencils usually are very soft, and the graphite breaks easily. Keep in mind that tones vary among manufacturers—one brand's HB may look very different from another brand's, so try to stick with one brand of pencil so your tones are consistent.

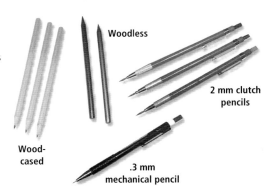

**Woodless**

**2 mm clutch pencils**

**Wood-cased**

**.3 mm mechanical pencil**

▼ **Sharpeners** Clutch pencils require special sharpeners, which you can find at art and craft stores. A regular handheld sharpener can be used for wood-cased and woodless pencils, but be sure to have several sharpeners on hand as these pencils can become dull. You also can purchase an electric sharpener, but it affords less control over the shape of the pencil tip.

▶ **Paper** The paper on which you choose to draw is as important as the pencil you use. Always buy the best paper you can afford, and make sure you buy plenty of it! Paper is classified by surface types and weight. *Hot-pressed* paper has a very smooth surface and accepts fine detail quite well. Most of the drawings in this book were done on hot-pressed paper. *Cold-pressed* paper has a rougher surface and provides built-in texture for your drawings. The heavier the weight of the paper, the thicker it is. Thicker papers are better for graphite drawings because they can withstand erasing far better than thinner papers can. For my finished works, I use 140-pound paper. (This weight refers to the entire ream, or 500 sheets, of paper.) Be sure to purchase acid-free paper, as acid causes paper to turn yellow over time.

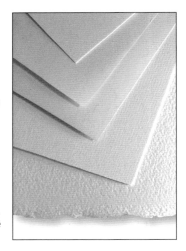

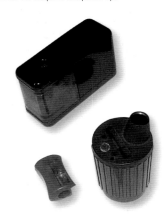

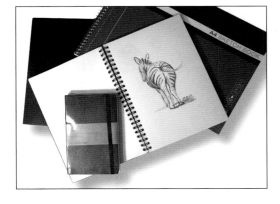

▶ **Sketchbooks** You can buy spiral-bound, stitched, or gum-bound sketchbooks in a variety of sizes. The paper in most sketchbooks is not designed for finished works—sketching is a form of visual note taking, and you should not worry about producing masterpieces with them. I keep a small notebook-sized sketchbook in my handbag so I can sketch whenever the mood strikes. I carry a larger sketchbook when I'm drawing on location.

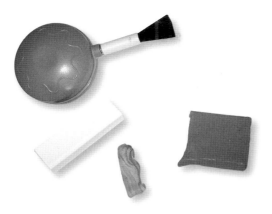

◄ **Erasers** I try to avoid erasing as much as possible, as it will damage the surface of the paper. But mistakes are inevitable, so you'll want to have a few erasers on hand. White plastic art erasers are good for removing harder pencil marks and for erasing large areas. Be careful when using this type of eraser, as rubbing too hard will damage the surface of the paper. This eraser also leaves crumbs, so be sure to softly brush them away with a makeup or camera lens brush. Kneaded erasers are very pliable; you can mold them into different shapes. Instead of rubbing the kneaded eraser across the paper, gently dab at the area to remove or lighten tone. Another great erasing tool is adhesive putty, made for tacking posters to a wall. Like a kneaded eraser, it can be molded and won't damage the paper. It is very sticky, though, so don't leave it resting on your paper for any length of time or it could leave a mark.

▶ **Blending Tools** Paper stumps (also called "tortillons") are used to blend or smudge areas of graphite into a flat, even tone. Be careful when using blending tools, as they tend to push the graphite into the paper, making the area difficult to erase. Another good way to blend is to wrap a chamois cloth around your finger. Never use your finger alone for blending—your skin contains oils that could damage the paper.

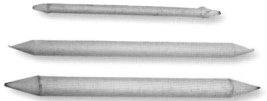

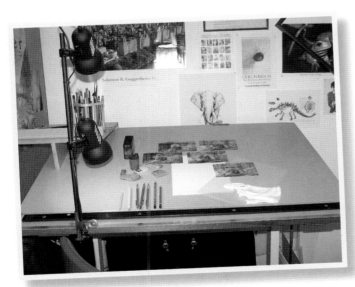

◄ **Workspace** You don't need a professional drafting table to start drawing—many brilliant drawings have been created on a kitchen table! You'll need a hard surface to use as a drawing board (or purchase a drawing board from an art supply store), and something to prop up the board with, such as a brick or a stack of books. Good lighting is essential—it's best to work in natural light, but you also can purchase a daylight bulb, which gives off a good white light and eliminates the yellow glare of standard bulbs. Make sure the lighting is direct and that there are no shadows falling across your work area. Also, you'll want to have a comfortable chair that supports your back.

## Protecting Your Work

*It's a good idea to use a hand shield to avoid smudging your work. You can simply tape a piece of paper on top of the areas you aren't working on or buy an inexpensive pair of cotton gloves and cut off the first three fingers to wear while you work. The cotton glove can still smudge your work if you are not careful, so you may want to use it in addition to the paper shield. Rotating your work as you draw is another good way to avoid smudges.*

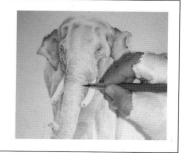

# GETTING STARTED

Experimenting and becoming familiar with your tools will make it easier for you to learn to draw. Play around with your pencils to see the different kinds of lines you can create, and practice doodling to learn how to control your strokes. Then experiment with different grades of pencils to create a variety of tones. The exercises on the next few pages will introduce you to your pencils and help you develop your hand/eye coordination.

## Doodling

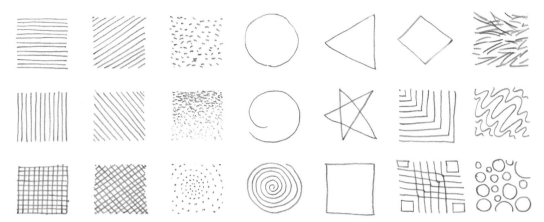

**Practicing Lines** On a sheet of hot-pressed paper, use an HB pencil to practice different lines, shapes, and doodles. Work slowly and precisely. Don't worry if your doodles start off a bit wobbly; you will improve your control with practice. When drawing shapes such as circles and triangles, try to make the shape with one continuous line (see page 9 for more information on this). After practicing lines and shapes for a while, try combining them to create various doodles. Get creative and create abstract designs. These simple doodles will help you get comfortable with your pencil, as well as discover how much pressure to apply to achieve a particular depth of tone (see "Experimenting with Tone" below). Try these exercises on different paper textures and compare the results.

## Experimenting with Tone

  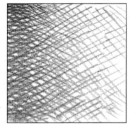 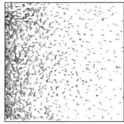

**Linear Strokes** Using the side of an HB pencil, draw a series of strokes in the same direction, each stroke slightly overlapping the previous one. Lift the pencil at the end of each stroke, slightly decreasing the pressure. Go back over your first layer two or three times to even out the tone. Alter the direction of the stroke to fill in any missed areas.

**Circular Strokes** Artists often use a circular motion to create large blocks of tone. Instead of drawing a series of lines, draw a series of small circles without lifting your pencil. I often go over linear strokes with circular strokes to even out the tone and fill in any missed areas.

**Crosshatching** Draw a series of parallel strokes (called "hatching"), and then add a layer of hatching in the opposite direction on top of the first layer. Strokes that are closer together create a darker tone; strokes that are father apart create a lighter tone.

**Pointillism** With this technique, you can create an area of tone with many small dots. Make the dots different sizes to create various tones and effects. Dots that are closer together create a darker area; dots that are farther apart create a lighter area.

# UNDERSTANDING VALUE

Now that you have some understanding of how to create solid tones with pencil, experiment with different grades of pencils to learn how to create variations in *value* (the relative lightness or darkness of a color or of black). By shading (adding dark values) and highlighting (adding light values), you produce the value variations that create the illusion of depth and dimension in your drawings, making them appear realistic.

| 2B | B | HB | H | 2H |
|----|----|----|----|----|

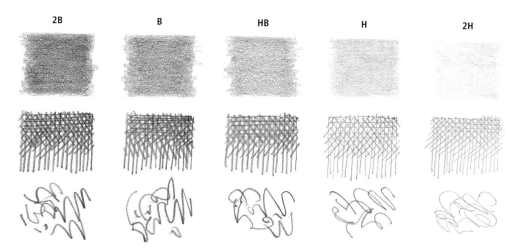

**Value Charts** Select a range of pencils from soft to hard (this chart uses 2B, B, HB, H, and 2H pencils). Use each pencil to create different techniques, such as linear strokes, crosshatching, and random lines. Use the same amount of pressure with each technique. When your chart is complete, label each different tone with the pencil you used. This chart will help you decide which pencil grades to use for different values and effects.

**Value Scale** Making your own value scale will help familiarize you with the different variations in value. Select a range of pencils (this scale was made with 2B, B, HB, H, and 2H pencils). Start with a 2B pencil to fill an area with horizontal, linear strokes. Then fill in the next areas with a B pencil. Continue in this manner until you create the lightest tone with the 2H pencil.

**Blended Value Scale** Now create a new value scale, this time blending the graphite with a tortillon to make an even, smooth gradation. Start at the far left with your 2B and work your way to the right, blending the graphite evenly to create a smooth texture. When you reach the lightest tones with your 2H, use a very light touch and even pressure to fade the tone off into the white of the paper.

# Working with Light and Shadow

Every shape or form we see is created by the reaction of the object's surface to light. To create a realistic image, the subject must be lit in a way that brings out its true form. For example, if you light an object from the front, you won't see the shadows that fall across the form, so it will appear flat. If you light the object from a three-quarter angle, the object will produce shadows; the transition in values will accentuate the object's dimension.

There are two main types of shadows: cast shadows and form shadows. *Cast shadows* are the shadows that the object throws onto other surfaces. *Form shadows* are the shadows that are on the surface of the object itself—these shadows give an object a sense of depth. Form shadows are dependent on the light source; they get darker as they move away from the light.

A drawing with a sharp contrast between light and shadow (very dark darks and very light lights) is considered a "high-contrast" work, whereas a drawing that uses mostly light and mid-range values is called a "low-contrast" work. Adding more contrast to your drawings will make the subject "pop" forward and look more three-dimensional, but you may want to use less contrast for "softer" subjects, such as a lioness nursing her cubs. Explore the difference between high- and low-contrast drawings by studying the examples below.

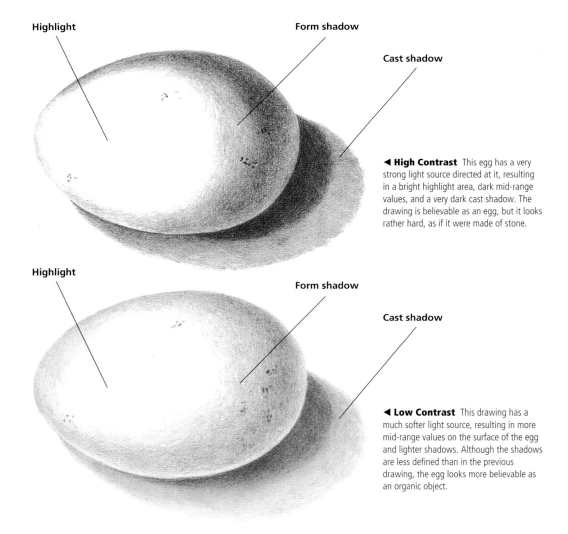

**Highlight**

**Form shadow**

**Cast shadow**

◀ **High Contrast** This egg has a very strong light source directed at it, resulting in a bright highlight area, dark mid-range values, and a very dark cast shadow. The drawing is believable as an egg, but it looks rather hard, as if it were made of stone.

**Highlight**

**Form shadow**

**Cast shadow**

◀ **Low Contrast** This drawing has a much softer light source, resulting in more mid-range values on the surface of the egg and lighter shadows. Although the shadows are less defined than in the previous drawing, the egg looks more believable as an organic object.

# LEARNING TO "SEE"

When you first begin drawing, it is important that you learn to draw what you *really* see, not what you *think* you see. Often novice artists will make basic mistakes because *they* draw their preconceived idea of an object rather than what the object actually looks like. Over the next two pages, you'll find three easy exercises that will train your eye to "see" correctly: contour drawing, negative drawing, and gesture drawing. You'll need some sketch paper and an HB or 2B pencil for these exercises. Don't use an eraser—just keep drawing, even if you think you make a mistake.

## Contour Drawing

*Contour drawing* is essentially drawing the outline of a subject. Contour drawing uses *line* to describe the shape of a subject without worrying about value—the range of lights and darks that give an object dimension. Choose some simple objects to practice with, such as a key, a feather, or some cutlery. On a piece of sketch paper, draw a square about 6" x 6". Then closely observe the object you are going to draw. Look only at the edges and focus on the contour of the object. Choose your starting point and put your pencil in position within the square on your paper. Now draw the outline of the object, looking back and forth between the object and your paper as you draw. Take your time and try not to lift your pencil from the paper until you have finished the outline—you can double-back over a line if you'd like. Don't worry if your drawing overlaps the edges of the square. This is just a practice exercise, so your drawing doesn't have to be perfect.

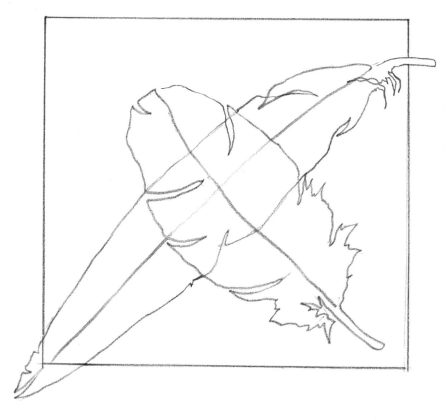

**◀ Using a Continuous Line**
In this contour drawing, I didn't worry about keeping the feathers inside the square. I drew each feather with one continuous line—even the spine of each feather is part of the same looping line.

# Negative Drawing

*Negative space* is the area that surrounds an object, and it is just as important as the object itself (the *positive space*). By drawing the area *around* an object, you can create the form of the object itself. This is called "negative drawing." To practice this, first draw a 6" x 6" square on your sketch paper. Look at your chosen object and observe the forms and shapes that are created around it. Without drawing an outline, start creating the negative areas around your subject with blocks of solid tone; the shape of your object will appear.

▶ **Recognizing the Subject** In this negative drawing, you can see that although there is no detail at all in the positive space, the shapes are still recognizable as feathers.

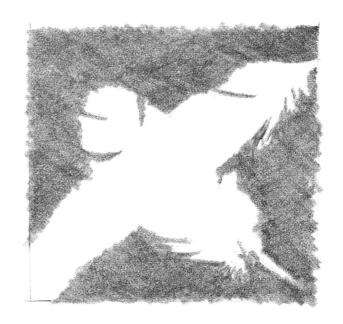

# Gesture Drawing

*Gesture drawing* is a fast, loose, expressive way of drawing. Although gesture drawings may not look very realistic, they often capture the essence of the subject. This is a wonderful way to depict movement when drawing animals from life; your eye takes a "snapshot" of the moving animal and quickly captures it on the page. To practice, draw another 6" x 6" square on your sketch paper. Study your object again for a minute or two. Is it small or large? Hard or soft? Your gesture drawing should reflect the essence of the object's form and texture. Using quick and deliberate marks, draw the object as completely and as accurately as you can with just a few lines and a little tone. Don't erase anything—if you aren't pleased with your drawing, just make another one.

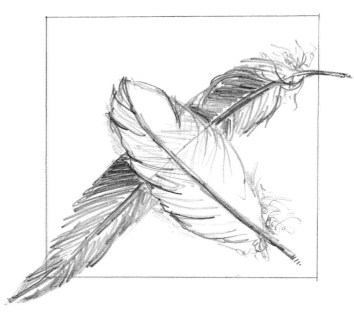

**Drawing Quickly** The gesture drawing shown here took less than a minute to create.

# DRAWING ACCURATELY

Accuracy is essential to drawing lifelike animals. If you are drawing in a more impressionistic manner, clinical accuracy is not as important—but your drawing must still retain a degree of reality to convince the viewer that your drawing is believable. Below are three different methods you can use to render the profile of a lioness with believable accuracy.

## Drawing Freehand

Freehand drawing is a skill that every artist needs to develop and practice, as it helps you observe and understand the form and structure of your subject. The more you practice, the better you will become. I always start my freehand work by observing and then breaking down the subject into simple shapes and measurement guidelines.

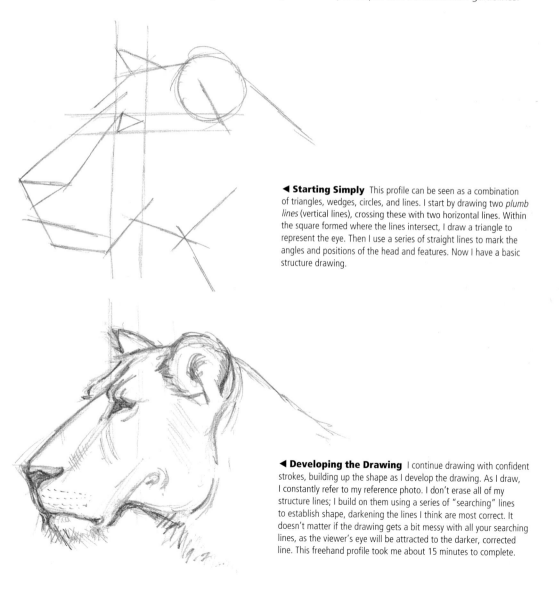

◄ **Starting Simply** This profile can be seen as a combination of triangles, wedges, circles, and lines. I start by drawing two *plumb lines* (vertical lines), crossing these with two horizontal lines. Within the square formed where the lines intersect, I draw a triangle to represent the eye. Then I use a series of straight lines to mark the angles and positions of the head and features. Now I have a basic structure drawing.

◄ **Developing the Drawing** I continue drawing with confident strokes, building up the shape as I develop the drawing. As I draw, I constantly refer to my reference photo. I don't erase all of my structure lines; I build on them using a series of "searching" lines to establish shape, darkening the lines I think are most correct. It doesn't matter if the drawing gets a bit messy with all your searching lines, as the viewer's eye will be attracted to the darker, corrected line. This freehand profile took me about 15 minutes to complete.

# Tracing and Grid Methods

Although freehand drawing is a good way to get to know the animal's form and represent it accurately, the quickest way to achieve perfect accuracy is to use either the tracing or grid methods. Neither of these methods should be considered "cheating": both are respected tools that have been used by artists for centuries. Using these methods will give you a perfect outline, but it is up to you to create the composition and final drawing with skill and technique. You also should never become too dependent on these methods; they shouldn't replace freehand drawing. Remember that any distortions in the photo (for example, due to wide-angle lenses) will translate to your drawing; you'll need to be prepared and willing to correct these distortions later.

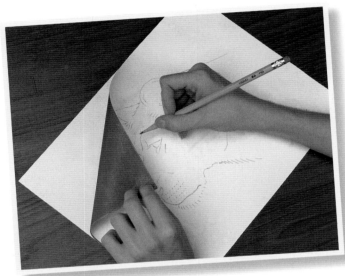

◄ **Tracing Method** Photocopy or print the image you wish to trace. (You may want to enlarge or reduce the image to the desired size.) Then tape a sheet of tracing paper on top of the image, and use a light table to help you carefully trace the outline of the animal, as well as the major facial features. If you don't have a light table, you can create your own transfer paper. Turn over the tracing paper and cover the back with an even layer of graphite. Then place the tracing paper (graphite-side down) on top of your final drawing paper. Use an HB pencil and carefully go over the lines on the tracing paper; the lines will transfer to the drawing paper below.

▶ **Grid Method** Make a photocopy of the reference photo, and then draw a grid of squares (1" x 1" is a good size to start with) on the photocopy. Next draw a corresponding grid on a piece of sketch paper. (Some artists draw their grids directly onto the final drawing paper, but I find this messy, and erasing the lines damages to the paper.) Make sure both grids have the exact same number of squares, even if the squares are different sizes—this ensures correct proportions. Once you've created the grids, simply draw what you see in each square of the reference in each square of the second grid. Draw in one square at a time until you have filled in all the squares. Now use the tracing method described above to transfer the drawing to your final paper.

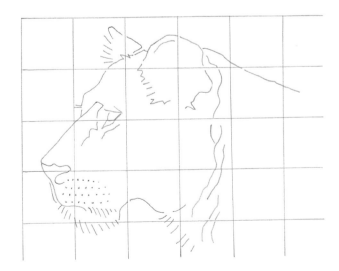

# PERSPECTIVE BASICS

For a drawing to be considered realistic, it needs to give the impression that it inhabits a three-dimensional space with depth and distance. To do this, employ the rules of perspective in your drawings. The first (and most important) rule of perspective is that objects that are closest to the viewer are larger than objects that are farther away. Here you'll find demonstrations of one- and two-point perspective; for more information, see William F. Powell's book *Perspective* (AL13) in Walter Foster's Artist's Library series.

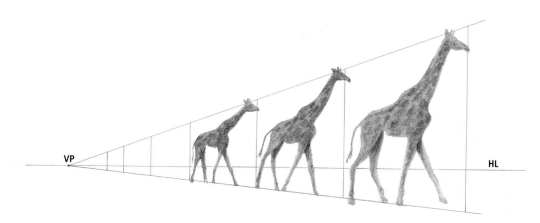

**One-Point Perspective** In one-point perspective, there is only one *vanishing point* (VP), or the point at which all perspective lines converge and seem to vanish. First draw a horizontal line on your paper to represent the horizon line (HL), or eye level. Then place a dot to the far left on the HL for the VP. Next draw a vertical line to the far right that intersects the HL at a 90-degree angle. About three-quarters of this line should be above the HL, and about one-quarter should be below it. Imagine that this vertical line is a fencepost (or a standing giraffe). Now draw a line from the top of this post to the VP, and another from the bottom of the post to the VP. This V-shaped guide allows you to see exactly where the top and bottom of each successive post (or giraffe) is located.

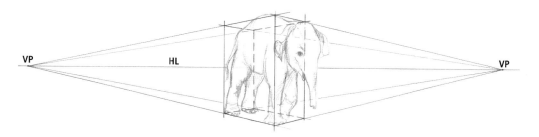

**Two-Point Perspective** In two-point perspective, there are two vanishing points. The best way to demonstrate this is by drawing a three-dimensional cube. First draw an HL, and place one VP on the far left and another VP on the far right. Draw a 90-degree line that bisects the HL at about the halfway point for the center "post." This line should extend above and below the HL at an equal distance. Draw lines from the top and bottom of the post that extend to each VP. Draw two more vertical lines to the left and right of the center post. These two new posts represent the corners of your cube. At the point where each corner post intersects the VP lines, draw a new line back to the opposite VP. These lines form the back edges of your cube, and the place where they intersect guides you to the position of the final back corner post, completing your cube. I sketched a baby elephant in my cube to demonstrate how animals are affected by perspective. The elephant's feet are positioned on the bottom corners of the cube, and the perspective of the VPs directly affects their positions.

# Foreshortening

Foreshortening is an important method of creating the illusion of depth in a drawing, and it works hand in hand with perspective in that the part of the subject that is closest to the viewer appears larger than the parts that are farther away. To create this illusion when drawing, just shorten the lines on the sides of the object that is closest to the viewer.

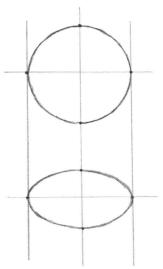

▶ **Visual Example**  To see foreshortening in action, hold a dinner plate straight out in front of you. It appears as a circle. Now tilt the plate slowly away from you. The plate now appears much shorter; this shape is called an "ellipse."

▼ **Recognizing Foreshortening**  This sketch of an iguana is a good example of foreshortening. Notice the difference in the size of the iguana's right foot compared to its left foot. The left foot was drawn much larger because it's closer to the viewer.

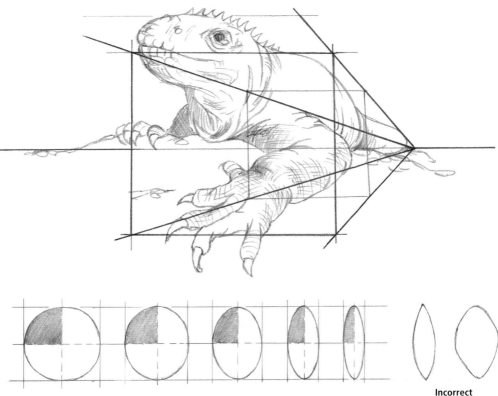

**Incorrect**

**Drawing Ellipses**  An ellipse is merely a circle that has been foreshortened, as discussed above. It's important for artists to be able to correctly draw an ellipse, as it is one of the most basic shapes used in drawing. Try drawing a series of ellipses, as shown here. Start by drawing a perfect square; then bisect it with a horizontal line and a vertical line. Extend the horizontal lines created by the top and bottom of the square; also extend the center horizontal line to the far right. Create a series of rectangles that reduce in width along the horizontal line. Go back to the square and draw a curve from point to point in one of the quarters, as shown here. Repeat this same curve in the remaining quarters (turn the paper as you draw if it helps), and you will have created a perfect circle within the square. Repeat this process in each of the narrowing rectangles to produce a range of ellipses. Use this exercise whenever you have difficulty drawing a symmetrical ellipse or circle.

# ANIMAL ANATOMY

To draw an animal in a believable way, you must thoroughly understand its underlying structure. By becoming familiar with the basic skeletal structure of a species, you can gain a better understanding of the form, movement, and posture of that animal. Drawing skeletons also helps you understand how and why a certain feature looks the way it does. The skeletal structure holds the muscles in place, and this affects how the skin and hair flow over the body.

## Studying Different Species

Drawing a range of animal structures helps you recognize the subtle differences in shapes among different species. For example, a canine's head posture is quite different from a feline's, as you can see in the following examples. Studying each of the basic structures here will help you draw all varieties of a species. For example, a tiger is similar to a very large house cat; a wolf is similar to a dog; a horse is similar to a zebra; and a wallaby is similar to a kangaroo. Once you understand the basic underlying structures, you easily can address differences in size and breeds.

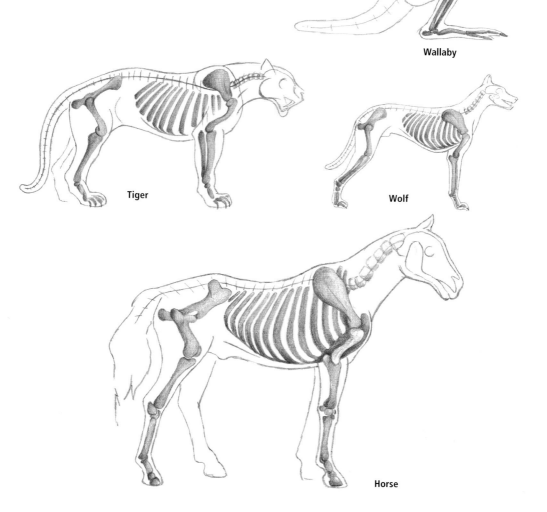

**Wallaby**

**Tiger**

**Wolf**

**Horse**

15

# ANIMAL TEXTURES

Once you have a basic understanding of an animal's skeletal structure, you must "clothe" it in either skin or hair. There is a vast range of textures you can create for skin and hair, and each requires a slightly different technique to achieve a realistic effect. Here I break down the process of drawing six different textures into steps so you can see how they are created. I use these techniques throughout the book, so you may want to refer to these pages when following the step-by-step projects.

## Short Fur

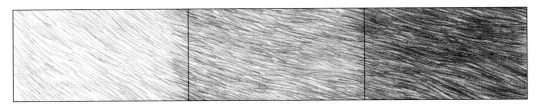

**Step 1** I create a light undercoat with a series of swift, short pencil strokes and a very sharp 2H .5 mm mechanical pencil. (Every pencil must be very sharp to achieve this effect.) I draw the strokes in the direction of the fur growth and avoid forming obvious patterns.

**Step 2** Now I use a sharp HB lead to create the second layer, using the same technique as in step 1. I don't fill in the entire area; instead I leave some of the paper showing through the lines for highlights.

**Step 3** I switch to a 2B pencil to work over the area again with the same short, swift strokes. This deepens the tone of the fur and creates a realistic texture. The darker 2B helps make the untouched areas "read" as lighter, individual hairs. This method is used for the kangaroo's fur on page 48.

## Short Patterned Fur

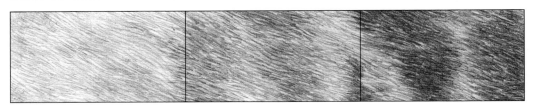

**Step 1** I use a blunt F pencil to fill in spots with very light, solid tone. Then I switch to a 2H pencil to work in a similar manner as in step 1 of "Short Fur" but build up dark areas by placing dark 2H strokes close together.

**Step 2** Now I switch to an HB pencil to make short strokes following the direction of fur growth. In the spotted areas, I keep the strokes close together; in the lighter areas, I keep the strokes farther apart. I leave some paper showing through for highlights.

**Step 3** I intensify the dark spots with a sharp 2B pencil and many closely placed strokes, varying the pressure on each stroke. I build up the tone a bit more in the lighter areas with a sharp HB. This technique is used for the tiger's fur on page 32.

## Long Hair

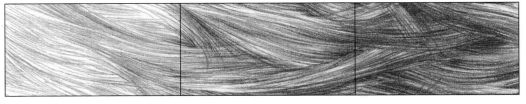

**Step 1** I use a very sharp HB .5 mm mechanical pencil to draw a series of long, curved strokes to make a "clump" of 20 to 30 lines. I draw all the lines in a clump in the same direction and at about the same length. Each clump varies in direction and length and often overlaps another clump.

**Step 2** As with the short fur, I use a sharp HB lead for the second layer, making my strokes more random than with the short fur. Again I leave areas of white showing through the strokes.

**Step 3** I switch to a 2B pencil to build up dark areas using long strokes. I create the darkest areas near the lightest lines and in areas where I want the deepest shadows. This contrast forms natural "hairs" and highlights. This method is used for the lion's mane on page 46.

## White Hair

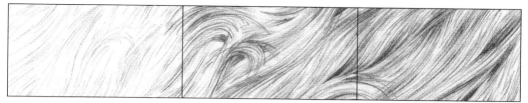

**Step 1** Many artists are intimidated by drawing white hair, but I love drawing it! The white of the paper does most of the work for you. You really only need to draw the shadows and the negative areas. I create the undercoat with a sharp 2H lead, but I lay down strokes only in the cast shadow areas. I keep my strokes very, very light.

**Step 2** With a sharp HB lead, I carefully create the shadows cast by the hairs, following the direction of hair growth. I don't draw too many lines, as I don't want to fill in all the white areas.

**Step 3** I switch to a sharp 2B to carefully create the darkest shadow areas. These dark values sharply contrast with the white of the paper, creating the illusion of white hair. Now I use the tip of the 2H to add some light strokes here and there to give the hair a little more definition. This technique is used in the lightest areas of the koala on page 36.

## Rough, Wrinkled Skin

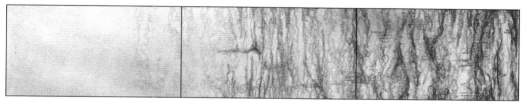

**Step 1** With a blunt F pencil, I lay down a light, even tone. Then I use a clean tortillon to blend and soften the tone, eliminating much of the "grain" of the paper. I try to keep some areas lighter and some darker so I don't create a flat tone.

**Step 2** To add wrinkles on top of the smooth tone, I use what I call a "scrumbling" technique. With a sharp 2H lead, I cover certain areas with a squiggly line that I make without lifting my pencil. This line sort of wanders about, creating the illusion of a bumpy texture. Then I switch to an HB to draw slightly darker horizontal lines over the scrumble lines. These lines of varying lengths represent the wrinkles.

**Step 3** Now I alternate between an HB and a 2B, adding more lines and scrumble lines over the first layer of tone. This loose technique works well for elephant, rhinoceros, and some reptile hides. It also can be used to create leathery effects for noses and footpads if the undercoat is created with a darker B pencil.

## Reptile Skin

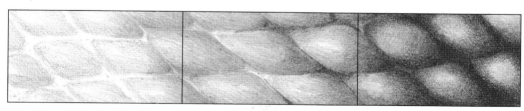

**Step 1** With a 2H pencil, I lightly draw a series of lines in one direction and another series of lines in the opposite direction to form a diamond pattern. I use a blunt F pencil to fill in each diamond with a series of lines placed close together. I leave a slight white outline and a highlight in the upper left corner of each diamond.

**Step 2** Switching back to the 2H, I stroke in the opposite direction on top of the layer of F strokes. This creates a blending effect without smudging the graphite with a tortillon. Now I add circular strokes with an HB in each diamond, concentrating on the lower right of each shape. I also use the HB to fill in the white outline around each diamond, creating a shadow between each shape.

**Step 3** Finally, I use a 2B to create the darkest shadow areas in the lower right of each diamond. Then I use an HB to add circular strokes over the previous layer, evening out the tone.

# DRAWING FROM LIFE

To draw animals realistically, it is important to observe them and sketch them from life. By watching how the animal moves and relates to its environment and other creatures, you can better portray the animal's character and appearance. Drawing an animal in the wild is difficult and possibly dangerous, so zoos, wildlife parks, animal sanctuaries, and rescue centers are the preferred source of subjects. If none of these are available to you, you can resort to a video, but this is a very poor second to seeing, hearing, and smelling the living creature.

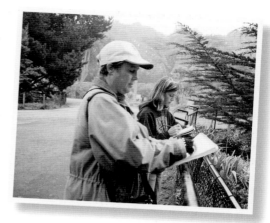

▶ **Drawing on Location** Author Linda Weil (left) sketches with her niece (right) at the San Francisco Zoo.

## What to Take

Your kit can be as simple or as complex as you wish and are capable of carrying. Here's a list of the items I always take when drawing on location:

1. A range of pencils (start with at least an HB and a 2B)
2. Sketchbook
3. Appropriate clothing and a hat
4. Insect repellent
5. Sunscreen
6. Water bottle
7. Pencil sharpener
8. Camera (if you're drawing an animal you've never seen before or don't have many references of)
9. Something to sit on (if you're going to be in front of one animal for an extended period)

## What to Do

1. **Be prepared for uncooperative animals.** It seems inevitable that whenever I go to study one particular animal, that is the ONE animal that is hidden all day or not on display. If I am after a particular animal, I have learned to always call first to ensure that the animal will at least be on display—whether it performs is a matter of luck. But there is nothing more frustrating than turning up on the one day of the year that the animal is getting its annual medical checkup and isn't on view!
2. **Be aware of the animal's habits.** Many animals are most active in the early morning or evening and will sleep out of sight in the afternoon. Is the animal nocturnal? If so, check with the keeper to find out the best time to view it, or arrange a private visit. Find out its feeding times and try to be there then.
3. **Be patient.** If the animal isn't moving or visible when you arrive, wait a while. Animals operate on their own schedules, not yours, so be patient and you will be rewarded.
4. **Be flexible.** Patience didn't work? Why not check out the animal next door? I guarantee you will see something interesting elsewhere if you keep your eyes open.
5. **Expect an audience.** People are always curious about what you are doing, especially children. If you are shy or hesitant about being watched, try to find a good spot that is discrete and out of the way. Some people will show great interest and ask questions about what you are doing. This is a wonderful opportunity for you to tell them about your artwork. If you are confident enough, give them your business card; you could be pleasantly surprised with a commission opportunity!
6. **Be polite.** Animals can be sensitive and shy, so don't shout or tap on the glass or wave your arms to attract the animal's attention. This can frighten the animal and make you look foolish, especially when the animal disdainfully ignores you! Also, don't hog the best viewing spots. Share these with the public, especially children. Do all you can to encourage their interest and allow them to see what you have been watching so carefully.

# Simplifying with Shapes

When you're just starting out, drawing animals from life can be very confusing. Often your first time drawing from life results in something that doesn't look anything like the animal in front of you. Don't be discouraged; you might just be drawing your preconceived notion of what the animal *should* look like instead of what it *really* looks like. The best way to avoid this is to make a deliberate effort not to draw the animal but, instead, to draw the shapes that compose the animal. By breaking down the animal into simple circles, ovals, squares, or triangles, you not only lessen the confusion, but you also make it easier to get the correct structure and proportions.

Below are several animal drawings that are made up of simplified shapes. As you can see, cylinders, circles, and ovals form the basic structure of each drawing. I often use this technique to begin a drawing. When you take your sketchbook out into the field and begin to draw, start with these simple shapes and lines. Work quickly and freely, and keep the drawing simple. Don't be worried if the animal is moving; just start another drawing on the same or next page. An animal usually will pace and return to its previous position so you can continue where the first or second drawing left off. Fill your page with several different views and angles of the moving animal. Don't fuss over small details; try to capture the overall form and feeling of the animal. Your aim is to take a quick "snapshot" in pencil.

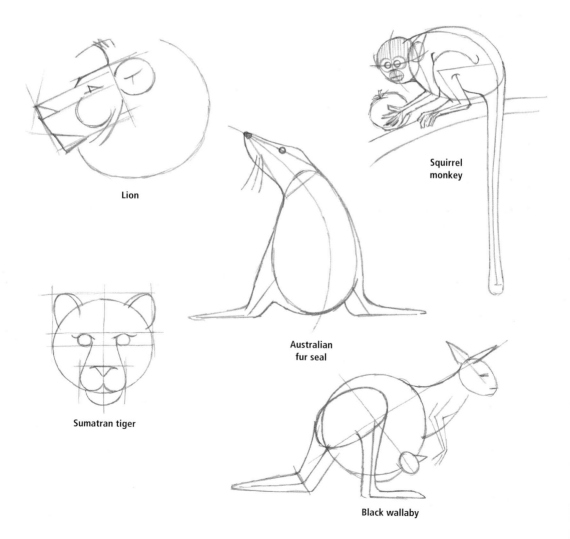

Lion

Squirrel monkey

Australian fur seal

Sumatran tiger

Black wallaby

# Sketchbook Selections

I frequently visit the local zoo and wildlife sanctuary. Whenever I go, I take my camera and sketchbook along. Sometimes I get so enthralled with watching the animals that I may do only one or two drawings. My books are filled with incomplete studies. My sketchbooks are not meant to be "finished" art but studies and observations of animal forms and behaviors. I never come away without having learned something. Here is a selection of drawings from my sketchbook that were made using the techniques discussed on page 19.

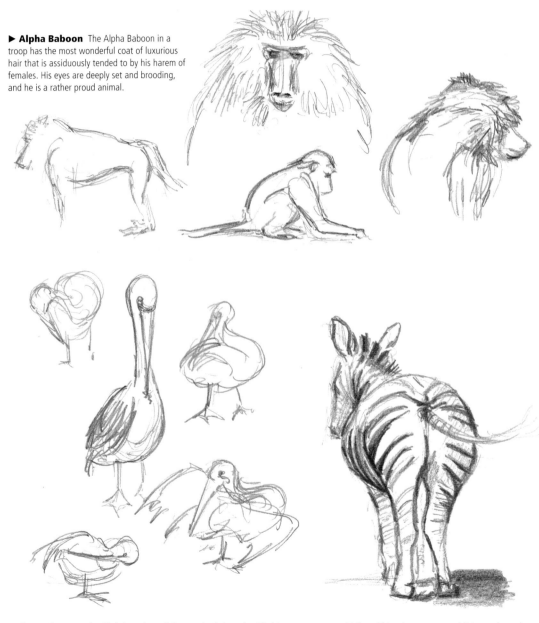

▶ **Alpha Baboon** The Alpha Baboon in a troop has the most wonderful coat of luxurious hair that is assiduously tended to by his harem of females. His eyes are deeply set and brooding, and he is a rather proud animal.

**Pelican** These preening birds have beautiful curves in their necks. I find it amazing that they can manipulate that huge beak so delicately to reach the most out-of-the-way areas on their bodies.

**Zebra** This zebra was most obliging and stood still for several minutes. He too was enjoying the spring warmth.

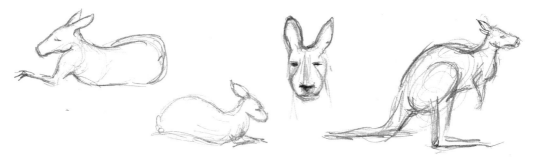

**Red Kangaroo** Called the "Old Man of the Desert," the kangaroo has a big, blocky head with large, upright ears and is heavily muscled around the shoulders and forearms. The kangaroo is tall and graceful in movement and languid in repose.

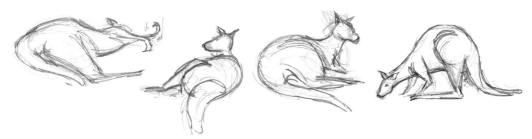

**Tamar Wallaby** Wallabies are very similar in structure to kangaroos. It is important to note the wallaby's smaller size, rounder body, and smaller head.

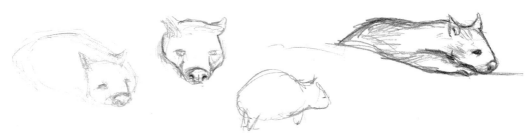

**Hairy-Nosed Wombat** Wombats often are called "bush bulldozers" because of their solid, sturdy, round bodies that can plow through almost anything.

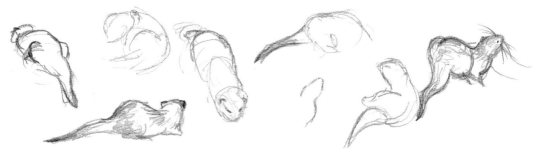

**Three-Clawed Otter** Otters are some of my favorite animals to draw, but they never sit still. They often return to similar positions, though, so I captured them progressively, drawing several different positions at once. This helped me successfully depict their wriggling bodies.

# COMPOSITION

*Composition,* or the arrangement of elements in a scene, can make or break a work of art. All the skill in the world will not help you if your composition is dull and uninteresting. Some artists just seem to have a natural "talent" for composition, but in actuality, this talent stems from basic principles and trial and error. Be sure to think about your drawing and plan it before you start. All of my work is "drawn" in my head before I put pencil to paper. Make quick thumbnail sketches to work out any compositional issues ahead of time.

## Composition Techniques

Here you'll read about a few compositional tricks I have practiced over the years. Remember that it's okay to make errors as long as you keep trying. If you feel uncomfortable with a drawing, try looking at it upside down or in a mirror; whatever is bothering you will be more easily apparent. Keep everything you draw; you can learn from your mistakes and lessen the chance of repeating them by reviewing less successful drawings every now and then.

### Odd Numbers and Asymmetry

Generally, subjects are more appealing when grouped in odd numbers rather than even numbers. Consider this when planning your composition. You can use even numbers in your compositions, of course, but you'll want the subjects to differ in size—for instance, you could draw three baby birds in a nest with their mother. Or you can introduce some asymmetry, like drawing three frogs on one end of a log looking at a solitary frog on the other end.

### The Rule of Thirds

Another method for creating a pleasing composition is to divide the picture into thirds (vertically or horizontally or both) and place your center of interest at or near one of the points where the lines intersect. This keeps your focal point away from the extremes—corners, dead center, or at the very top or bottom of the composition. In this drawing, the tiger's right eye is placed where two of the lines intersect, creating a pleasing composition.

### Geometric Composition

Divide the composition into geometric shapes (rectangles, triangles, or circles), and place the elements of the drawing where these lines divide and intersect, as well as within the areas created by the intersections. Look at the geometric shapes that form in your drawing. Is there a strong triangular formation? Or have you created a centrally balanced work? Notice how the internal shapes lead your eye around the page. Be aware of any compositional subtleties that can create divisions in your drawing.

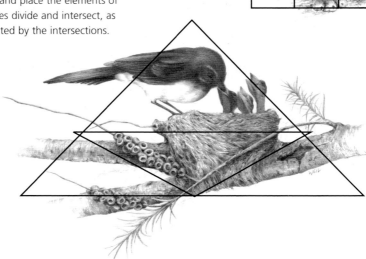

## Using References

When planning a composition, use as many different types of references as you can to explore your subject. I base most of my work on sketches and photos I have taken. I also source information from the Internet, magazines, books, and other photographs. Be aware that photos taken with a flash will be tonally flat and contain flash highlights, especially in the eyes. For this reason, don't copy a photograph exactly; just use it as a guide.

Whenever you use material that is not your own, you must be aware of copyright restrictions. If you have used another's work to create your drawing, you cannot sell or publish that work as an original. My advice is that if you are in doubt, ask the original creator's permission first. Many photographers and artists will grant you permission, but some will require a fee.

## Using Photo-Editing Software

If I want to combine elements from multiple photographs into one image, I can use photo-editing software to physically piece together the photographs. Below I demonstrate how I used several different references to create the composition on page 61. I had taken a number of excellent shots of a group of meerkats, but none of the shots had the animals all looking in one direction. I wanted the drawing to show all the animals huddled together, making eye contact with the viewer. To do this required cutting and pasting from three separate photos.

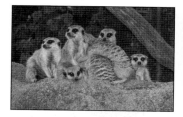

**1** This is my base photo. The body positions are pretty much how I want them, but only two of the animals are looking directly at the camera.

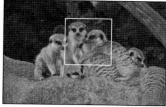

**2** I like the heads of the top two meerkats from the second photo (shown here), so I select and copy them.

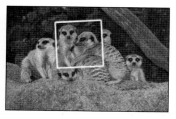

**3** I paste the new heads onto a new layer in my file. This obscures the head of the back meerkat, though. To fix this, I return to the first layer, and select and copy the back meerkat's head.

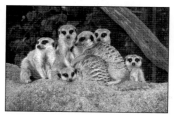

**4** I paste the new back head onto a new layer in my working file, erasing any part of the image that covers up the front meerkat.

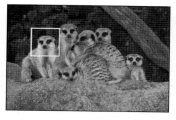

**5** Next I select the head of the far-left meerkat from the third photo (shown here) and copy it. Then I paste the head onto a new layer.

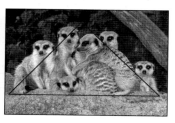

**6** I manipulate the pasted images in each layer until I'm happy. I like the triangular composition created by the meerkats. I save this as a new final file.

# ASIAN ELEPHANT

Large animals such as elephants are great subjects for your first attempts at drawing wildlife. The big, round forms are easy to understand, and the texture of the skin is less daunting than fur. This project features an Asian elephant, which differs slightly from an African elephant in that it has a smaller body and ears, as well as a more rounded back. It also has a fourth toenail on its rear feet and only one "finger" at the end of its trunk. The head and body are sparsely covered in wiry hair. Because they are working animals, their tusks often have been cut short to prevent damage to their surroundings. Noting these characteristics will help you accurately portray this type of elephant.

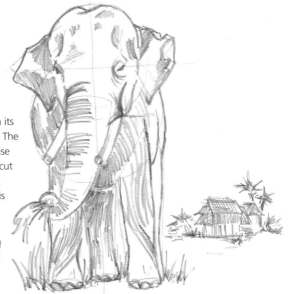

▶ **Rough Sketch** I start with a rough sketch as a plan for the final drawing. Using a soft 2B pencil, I define the general forms of the elephant. I also indicate the lights and darks, keeping in mind that the light is coming from above right. I want the viewer to know that this elephant is Asian, so I decide to add a Malaysian-style house in the background.

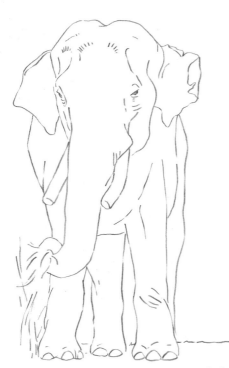

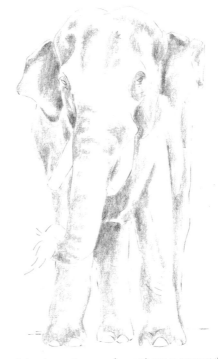

**Step 1** Now I transfer only the outline of my sketch to my final art paper. I tape the sketch to a bright window and place a piece of art paper over the sketch. Then I use an HB pencil to carefully trace the outline on the art paper. I do not include any details or the background at this time. For reproduction purposes, the outline you see here is much darker than I would use in my work. I will erase much of the outline by dabbing at it with a kneaded eraser as I work.

**Step 2** I need to create a very soft, smooth tone to represent the underlayer of skin prior to adding the rough, cracked texture. Using a 2B woodless pencil, I make small circular strokes to fill in the darkest shadow areas. I leave large areas of white, as I will blend the graphite into these areas in the next step. To help protect the white of the paper, I wear a cotton glove with the tips of the fingers cut off. I also rest my hand on a sheet of paper that covers part of the drawing surface.

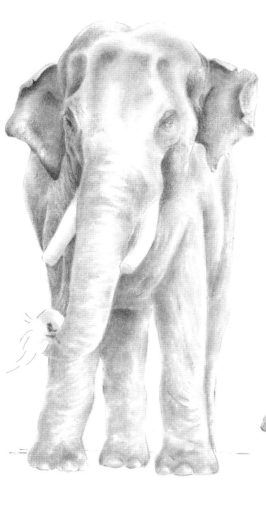

◄ **Step 3** Using a tortillon and light, circular motions, I slowly blend the dark graphite into the white areas of the paper for a smooth, satiny look. I use this residual graphite on the tip of the tortillon to "paint" lighter tones over the white areas of the elephant. Then I use a 2B and circular motions to darken the shadows from step 2.

► **Step 4** I use the graphite on the tip of the tortillon to "paint" softer tones into the whites of the tusks, across the forehead and ears, and on the trunk and chest to form ridges and folds of skin. Working over the head, ears, and a bit of the trunk, I add some wrinkles using a sharp HB mechanical pencil. I sharpen the edges of the curls in the ears and use circular strokes around the eyes and brows. Then I continue down the body, adding wrinkles and creases. I refer to my reference to see how the wrinkles flow over the legs. I add details to the toes and trunk, and I darken the ends of the tusks. I blend this linework slightly with a tortillon. I realize that something is not quite right with the legs, but I keep drawing. Using a sharp 2B mechanical pencil, I further darken and enhance the wrinkles, as well as areas around the eyes and inside the ears. I use adhesive putty to lift out tone from the outward side of the elephant's front left leg, as well as areas on the head and trunk.

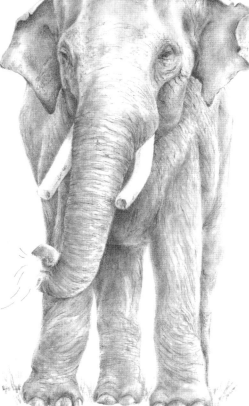

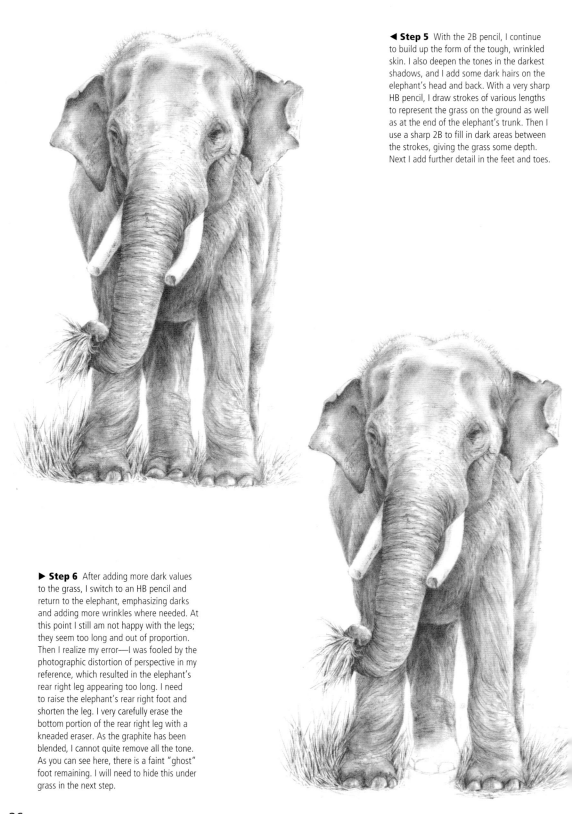

**◄ Step 5** With the 2B pencil, I continue to build up the form of the tough, wrinkled skin. I also deepen the tones in the darkest shadows, and I add some dark hairs on the elephant's head and back. With a very sharp HB pencil, I draw strokes of various lengths to represent the grass on the ground as well as at the end of the elephant's trunk. Then I use a sharp 2B to fill in dark areas between the strokes, giving the grass some depth. Next I add further detail in the feet and toes.

**► Step 6** After adding more dark values to the grass, I switch to an HB pencil and return to the elephant, emphasizing darks and adding more wrinkles where needed. At this point I still am not happy with the legs; they seem too long and out of proportion. Then I realize my error—I was fooled by the photographic distortion of perspective in my reference, which resulted in the elephant's rear right leg appearing too long. I need to raise the elephant's rear right foot and shorten the leg. I very carefully erase the bottom portion of the rear right leg with a kneaded eraser. As the graphite has been blended, I cannot quite remove all the tone. As you can see here, there is a faint "ghost" foot remaining. I will need to hide this under grass in the next step.

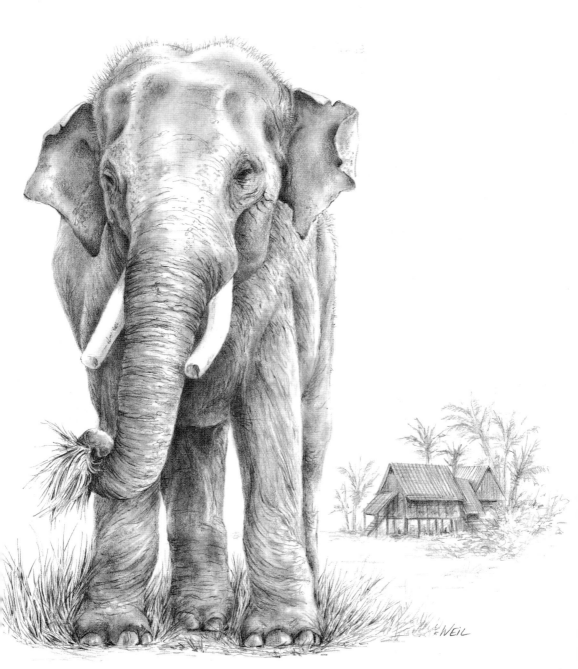

**Step 7** I lightly redraw the foot, setting it back farther in the picture. Then I draw grass over the areas of the original foot that I couldn't entirely erase. Now I turn my attention to the background, using an F pencil to draw the shapes of the house freehand. Then I sketch some palm trees and vegetation around the house. After switching to an HB pencil to develop the details of the house and vegetation, my drawing is complete. Overall, I'm happy with the drawing; I like how the animal is placed in an environment that identifies its location and also hints at its working life. The correction to the length of the back leg has certainly improved the work.

# AUSTRALIAN BARKING OWL

The large, slightly crossed eyes and facial "mask" of the Australian Barking Owl are particularly striking. I visited a local wildlife sanctuary and closely observed this subject during a "free flight" demonstration. I was able to take a number of good photos of the bird in flight, as well as when it landed on a nearby fence railing, which is the pose I choose to depict. As I have mentioned, it is always helpful to understand the anatomy of the animal you are drawing. When drawing birds, pay attention to the way the feathers lay. Most birds share the same general feather structure, so refer to diagrams in encyclopedias or other references for help.

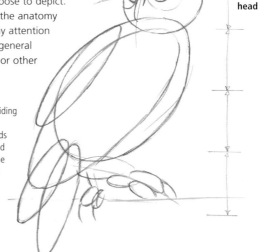

1 head

▶ **Basic Shapes** I start by drawing a simple circle for the head, dividing it horizontally and vertically along arcs that represent the curvature of the head. My photos show that the owl's body is approximately 2 heads high, the wings extend to about $2^1/2$ heads, and the tail feathers extend to about $3^1/2$ heads. I use these proportions to determine the size of the remaining basic oval shapes that represent the owl's body. Then I find the placement of the eyes and beak and sketch them.

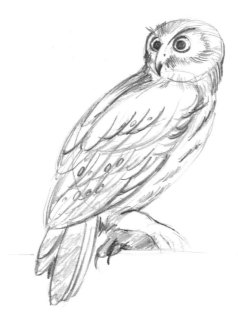

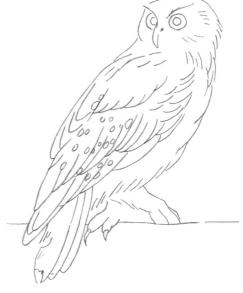

**Rough Sketch** Now I develop the basic shapes to create a sketch for my final drawing. Using an HB pencil, I quickly sketch in and define the forms. I delineate the individual feathers on the wings and tail, and I outline the feather directions on the face and chest.

**Step 1** When I'm happy with my sketch, I place a piece of tracing paper over the sketch and carefully trace the outline and major features. I attempt this four times before I'm satisfied that all the elements are correctly positioned. Then I transfer the final outline onto my art paper with the help of a light box. Notice that the eyes appear slightly distorted in the final sketch. Many artists use a circle template to draw eyes, but I prefer to draw them freehand so they aren't too perfect, thus appearing more realistic.

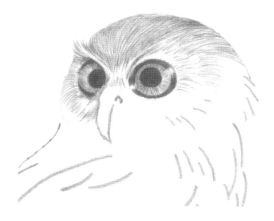

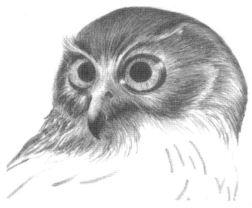

**Step 2** Starting with the iris, I use an H pencil to lightly draw a series of lines that radiate from the pupil. Then I use a 2B pencil and circular strokes to fill in the pupil. After sharpening my 2B, I darken areas around the eyeball to create this bird's "eyeliner" effect. I am very careful to keep the highlights in the bird's left eye white, as I'd rather work around the white of the paper than lift out tone later. I feel that the pupil is a bit small, so I enlarge it slightly with a sharp 2B pencil. Then I add light tone to the iris using H and HB pencils. With the H pencil I create curved strokes on the head and around the eyes, always drawing in the direction that the feathers lay.

**Step 3** To achieve the smooth, sleek texture of the feathers, I layer over my H strokes with sharp 2B and HB pencils. I continue layering feathers across the lower area of the face and around the beak with H, HB, and 2B pencils. Where the feathers are lighter, I use an H pencil and less pressure. I layer HB and 2B strokes to create darker tones. Moving to the bottom of the beak, I layer circular strokes with a 2B to create the dark tip. Then I add circular HB strokes along the side of the beak and blend the tone lightly into the white areas of the beak. With the sharp 2B, I darken the nasal holes and the outline of the beak. Then I layer more lines across the cheeks.

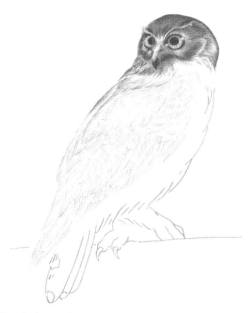

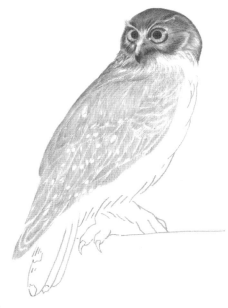

**Step 4** I'm pretty happy with the way the head looks, so now I focus on the body. I start by lightly dabbing at the outline with a kneaded eraser to lighten it. Then I work on the feather shapes with a very sharp HB pencil, making sure that the strokes always reflect the proper direction of the feathers. These HB strokes create the underlayer for the feathers and dictate the direction of all subsequent strokes. Working down the wing, I am careful to leave the white spots and markings free of tone.

**Step 5** Now I use a sharp 2H pencil to layer strokes on top of the previous HB strokes, smoothing and evening the tone as I go. I make the 2B strokes the same length and use the same amount of pressure as with the HB, but I place the strokes much closer together. This creates an all-over gray tone, but some of the previous HB strokes show through, giving the impression of a feather texture. I still leave the spots and markings free of tone, and I try to leave the edge of each feather white as well.

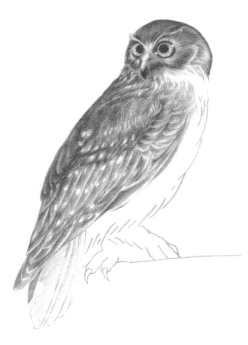

**◄ Step 6** As I deepen the tone on the body, I alternate between a 2B and an HB pencil. I use the 2B to create darker edges and shadows, and I use the HB to stroke on top of the previous layers, blending and evening out the tone. At this point I also draw some of the HB strokes in opposite directions, creating a bit of crosshatching on the feathers. After lightening the outline of the tail with a kneaded eraser, I create the HB underlayer for the feathers on the tail.

**► Step 7** I repeat step 6 on the tail feathers, adding a bit more crosshatching here than on the body. (If you closely observe a feather, you will see that refracted light shining across the veins gives the appearance of crosshatching.) Returning to the body, I use a slightly blunt F pencil and lightly stroke all over the previous layers of feathers, evening out the tone and darkening the other layers. After erasing the outline of the chest and torso with a kneaded eraser, I lightly stroke in the feathers on the chest. Because the light is directly hitting this side of the bird, I don't need to depict the edge with an outline—the suggestion of feathers will visually fill in the gaps to form the owl's chest and the left side of its body.

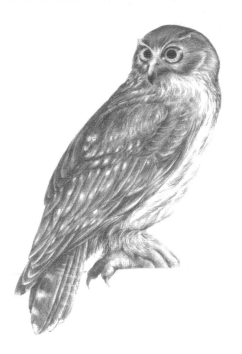

**◄ Step 8** I use a 2B pencil to darken the tail feathers, repeating steps 5 and 6. To create more white markings in the tail, I carefully lift out some tone with adhesive putty, forming light, horizontal stripes. Still using the sharp 2B, I darken some of the feathers on the chest. Then I use a blunt H pencil and circular strokes to create a very light base tone on the feet. To build up form on the feet, I add another layer of circular strokes with an HB pencil, and yet another layer with a 2B pencil. Switching to an F pencil, I add a fourth layer of circular strokes, lightly blending the previous layers. Then I use a very sharp 2B pencil to draw wrinkles on the feet, as well as darken the talons and the areas between the toes. I also add some darker strokes around the neck and under the wing.

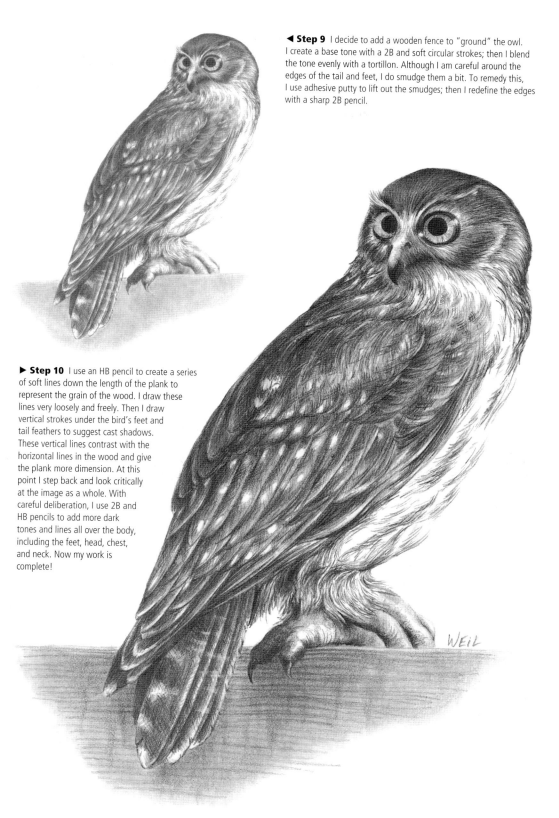

**Step 9** I decide to add a wooden fence to "ground" the owl. I create a base tone with a 2B and soft circular strokes; then I blend the tone evenly with a tortillon. Although I am careful around the edges of the tail and feet, I do smudge them a bit. To remedy this, I use adhesive putty to lift out the smudges; then I redefine the edges with a sharp 2B pencil.

**Step 10** I use an HB pencil to create a series of soft lines down the length of the plank to represent the grain of the wood. I draw these lines very loosely and freely. Then I draw vertical strokes under the bird's feet and tail feathers to suggest cast shadows. These vertical lines contrast with the horizontal lines in the wood and give the plank more dimension. At this point I step back and look critically at the image as a whole. With careful deliberation, I use 2B and HB pencils to add more dark tones and lines all over the body, including the feet, head, chest, and neck. Now my work is complete!

WEIL

# TIGER CUB

Young animals have specific traits that can be very engaging—large eyes and ears, fluffy fur, oversized feet, and gangly limbs. To accurately represent a young animal, it's important to observe the proportions of the head to the body when drawing, as these measurements are very different from an adult's. The success of your portrait will depend on the accuracy of the proportions. In this drawing, I employ the technique of negative drawing, as discussed on page 10. I also introduce the technique of incising, which allows you to create fine white lines in a dark area.

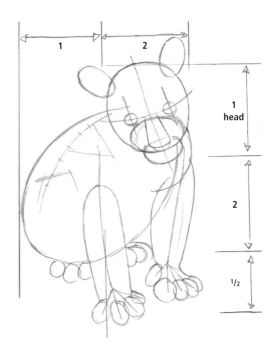

▶ **Basic Shapes** I start by drawing a circle for the head. After bisecting the circle vertically and horizontally, I block in the eyes on the curved horizontal line. Then I add ovals for the ears, as well as the muzzle. I add the bridge of the nose using a simple cylinder. Looking at my photo references, I see that the torso is about 2 heads wide. I use a larger oval for the torso. Then I block in the front legs and paws, remembering that the tiger is about 2¹⁄₂ heads tall.

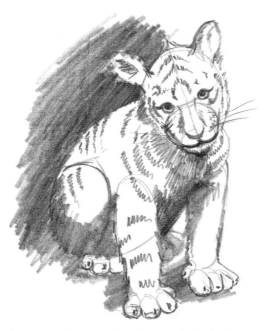

**Rough Sketch** Using my basic shapes as a guide, I sketch and define the facial features and other details with a 2B pencil. I constantly refer to my photographs to check positions and proportions. I decide that I want the cub to be lit dramatically, so I quickly add a dark background that also functions as a cast shadow. This background forms the edges of the cub's back and back leg (see step 2). Then I roughly place the stripes and shadow areas. Although very rough, this sketch familiarizes me with the subject and the chosen pose.

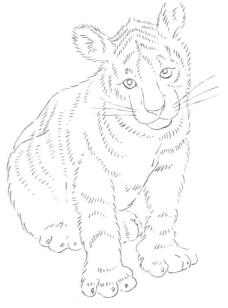

**Step 1** I place a piece of tracing paper over the sketch and carefully trace the outline of the body and major features. Then I use a light box to transfer the final outline onto my art paper. I indicate the stripes with short linear strokes. For reproduction purposes, the lines shown here are much darker than I usually draw them. As I draw, I will carefully erase the outlines with a kneaded eraser. I include the whiskers in my initial outline for placement, but I immediately erase them, instead impressing (or incising) them into the paper with a knitting needle. (See "Incising" on page 34.)

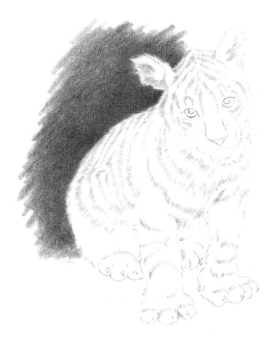

**◄ Step 2** There are few actual lines in nature; instead, shapes are formed by an object's reaction to light. To show this, I create a dark background that will form the edge of the tiger's back. This is an example of negative drawing. First I lightly erase the outline of the tiger's back from step 1. Then I hone the tip of a 2B woodless pencil by rubbing it on scrap paper. I draw broad, flat strokes to build up the background, leaving the edges loose and ragged. (See "Using Woodless Pencils" on page 35.) To even out the tone, I add a layer of circular strokes with an HB mechanical pencil. Next I use a sharp HB pencil and short strokes to draw the tiger's stripes.

**► Step 3** To even out the tone in the background, I add another layer of circular strokes with a blunt H pencil. This has the same effect as using a tortillon to blend tones. Now I use a very sharp 2B to develop the stripes further, using the same short strokes that follow the direction of fur growth. I also use the 2B to create the shadowed areas on the back leg, inside the ears, under the chin, and the area beneath the animal. I switch to a sharp HB pencil and place short fur strokes all over the cub's body, as well as more fur and shadowed areas in the ears.

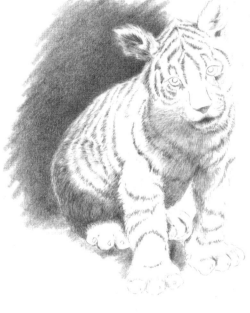

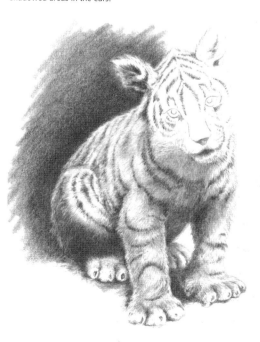

**◄ Step 4** With a sharp 2H pencil, I add layers of short strokes over the entire body, smoothing and blending the previous layers. I know I need to add several more layers of blended tone to the fur to make it appear soft and fluffy. After studying my reference photo again, I use a slightly blunt F pencil and layer very light, circular strokes on top of the shadowed areas of the coat. Then I use a 2B pencil to deepen the tone of the background, as well as the dark areas on the back leg and paws. I also use the sharp 2B to create darker areas in some of the stripes. I leave areas of the coat free of tone to create the strongest highlights. Then I use a very sharp HB pencil to add more short lines all over the body, enhancing the fur texture.

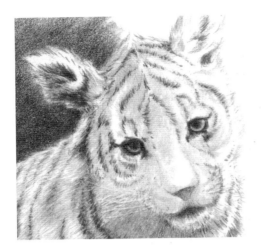

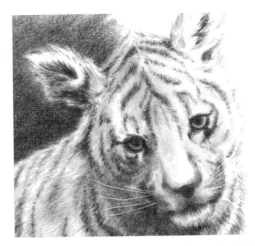

**Step 5** Now I use a sharp 2B to draw the dark, thick lines around the eyes, emphasizing the upward curve on the outer edges. I draw the pupil at the top of the eyeball to show an upward gaze. Then I draw lines that radiate from the pupil with a sharp 2H pencil. With an HB pencil, I add more strokes to the dark rings around the eyes. Then I add short, sharp 2H pencil strokes all over the top of the head and around the mouth to create more fur. I use a blunt F pencil to add circular strokes down the left side of the nose and over the muzzle.

**Step 6** Here I build up the shadow areas on the left side of the face and under the chin to create form. I do this with the 2B pencil and circular strokes. I also use this pencil to darken the tip of the nose, as well as the soft fur around the mouth. Notice how the incised whiskers really start to stand out. After sharpening the 2B, I use it to carefully darken some of the stripes on the head using short strokes. I also add more detail on the ears, using the 2B to "cut" into the white area of the paper, which forms little white hairs.

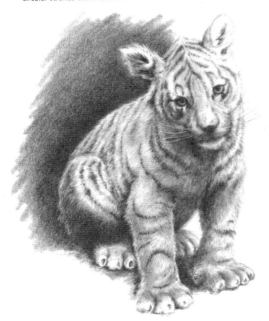

**Step 7** After taking a step back, I decide to add more contrast by creating darker fur in places. I don't want to overwork the drawing and lose the detail, though, so I sharpen the HB pencil almost every fifth or sixth stroke to keep my lines crisp. I slowly build up the linework around the mouth, ears, and neck. I also pick out the underside of the incised whiskers, giving them a bit more form and dimension. With a blunt F pencil, I add some circular strokes to the paws, creating a soft tone. Then I use the 2B pencil to add shadows between and underneath the toes, as well as to darken the claws.

## Incising

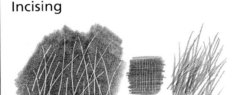

*It is very difficult to create fine white lines in areas where you have already added tone. An easy way to create white lines is to indent them into the paper before you start drawing. This is called "incising." Use a smooth, slightly blunt object such as a knitting needle, but make sure the point is not too sharp. Once you've visualized where your white lines will appear, "draw" the lines with your implement, using a steady pressure that is hard enough to indent the paper but not hard enough to gouge it. Pay attention to where you have already indented, as the lines quickly seem to become invisible. When you draw over the incised area, the graphite will "skip" over the indentations and leave behind clean white lines, as shown in the examples here.*

34

▶ **Step 8** Now it's time to add final details. Using a woodless 2B pencil, I draw some loose scrumble lines around the tiger's paws. (See page 17 for more on scrumbling.) I don't try to create any detail here; I just want to give the impression that the tiger is sitting on some loose leaf litter. I hold my pencil loosely and at a slight angle as I scrumble. I am careful to keep the division where the ground meets the paws crisp and sharp. Finally, I return to my sharp HB pencil and work over the entire drawing one last time. I add a bit more detail to the claws; build up some more fur around the neck, both sides of the face, and around the ears; add a bit more tone to the back paw to make it recede more; and refine the fur on the toes and around the mouth. I decide that any more "tweaking" will overwork the drawing, so I declare it finished by signing my name.

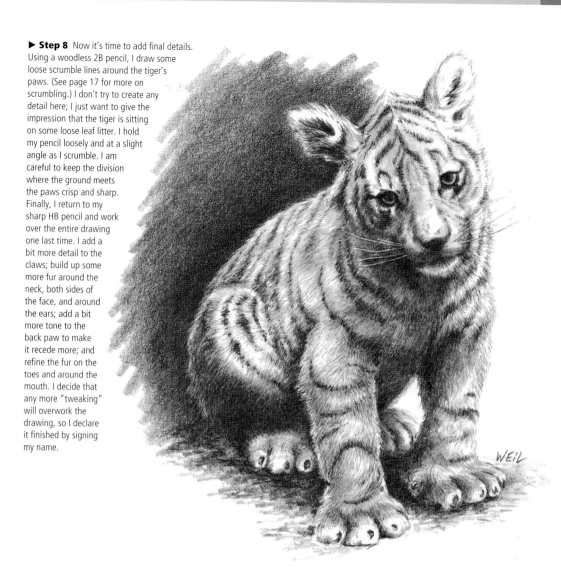

## Using Woodless Pencils

*A woodless pencil is a solid core of graphite covered with a thin sheath of plastic. It is great for creating broad areas of tone (such as the background of this drawing) or for making quick gesture sketches. You can achieve different results by holding the pencil at different angles to the paper. By holding the barrel lower to the paper and using more of the side of the lead, you'll create a broader stroke. The more upright you hold the pencil, the finer the lines become.*

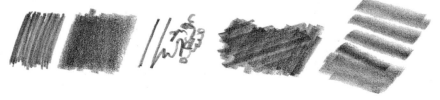

# KOALA

Koalas are one of my favorite subjects to draw. Their faces have such character, and their simple, round bodies are easy to draw freehand. Koalas don't move about much—in fact, they sleep more than 18 hours a day! So if you see a koala awake, be sure to take a photo because it is a rare opportunity.

When drawing a koala, you will need to use a number of pencil techniques to create short and long fur, white and dark fur, and the varied textures of the nose, claws, and eyes.

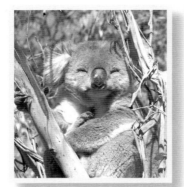
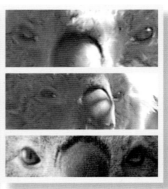

**Taking Multiple Photos** I spent several days taking photos at a local koala sanctuary, but I couldn't get a "perfect" shot. The best-posed animals were asleep or squinting, and those with their eyes open were in awkward positions. So I took as many photos as I could of koalas both asleep and awake, and I combined multiple references for the final composition.

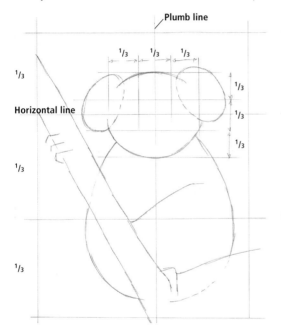

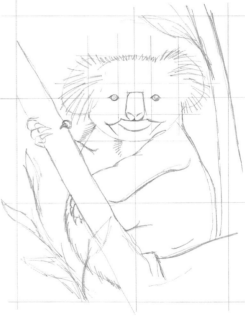

**Finding the Proportions** To figure out the correct proportions of the koala, I first draw a 6.5" x 9" rectangle on a sheet of tracing paper. I divide this shape horizontally into thirds; then I draw a vertical plumb line that is slightly off-center down the length of the rectangle. Referring to my main reference photo for the scale and size of the head, I center the head circle exactly where the plumb line and the first horizontal line meet. Then I roughly divide the head circle into thirds horizontally and vertically—this will help me correctly position the facial features. I do not need to use a ruler to measure this; I just use my eyes to judge the correct distances. Now I use simple oval shapes to block in the round shapes of the body and ears. Using my reference as a guide, I sketch the arms, fingers, and tree branches.

**Blocking in the Features** Now that I have the proportions down, I place another sheet of tracing paper over my drawing and begin refining the shape of the koala. Constantly referring to my main reference shot, I block in the nose, noting where it starts and finishes in relation to the grid. Using my other reference shots as a guide, I position the open eyes almost exactly on the top horizontal line of the grid. Now I place the mouth and cheeks, which are a series of arcs within the bottom third of the head circle. I build up some fur in the ears, on top of the head, and on the chest; then I develop the arms and legs, adding the long claws and noting where the heel of the foot rests against the upright branch. I decide to omit the back foot that awkwardly overlaps the chest area in the main reference photo. I know enough about koalas to know that my drawing will be believable if the foot is tucked out of sight behind the branch. Finally, I add a few more tree branches and leaves.

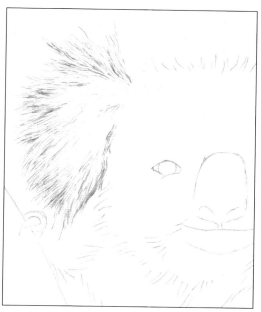

◄ **Step 1** After transferring the outlines of my sketch to a piece of 300 gsm (140 lb) hot-pressed paper, I start developing the ear on the left, as I plan to work down and across to the right. First I lighten the outline of the ear with a kneaded eraser. Then I use a sharp 2H clutch pencil to draw long, smooth lines for the undercoat, varying their lengths and directions.

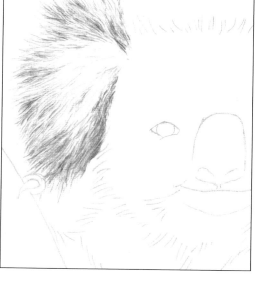

▶ **Step 2** I switch to an HB clutch pencil and draw more long, broken strokes around the 2H strokes, carefully leaving the paper white in areas. As I work in the dark strokes, the white of the paper begins to form the white hairs. (This is a form of negative drawing.)

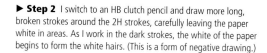

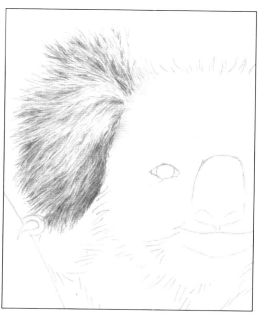

◄ **Step 3** Using a sharp 2B clutch pencil, I begin to intensify the shadowed areas of the fur under and on the edge of the ear. This dark tone creates a high contrast and makes the white areas stand out, increasing the impression of long, white fur. I return to the ear again with the 2H clutch pencil, refining and smoothing out the detail. By completing ear on the left first, I have established a value range for the rest of my drawing; the ear will act as a visual gauge.

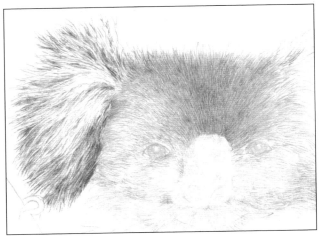

**◄ Step 4** After lightening the outline of the rest of the head with a kneaded eraser, I use a 2H clutch pencil to create short, quick strokes all over the head, avoiding the eyes and the nose. I draw in the direction of fur growth, placing my strokes very close together and using a tight, controlled movement. My wrist does not move at all; my fingers do all the work. When I've covered the face, I go back in with an HB pencil and darken the areas across the forehead and above the nose, using the same short strokes as before. Then I use a 2H to add a quick layer of fur to the ear on the right, as well as to build up the fur around the cheeks, chin, and mouth. I form the shape of the iris in the each eye with a light layer of 2H, and I add some tone to the nose.

**► Step 5** After dulling an HB pencil by rubbing it on a piece of scrap paper, I add circular strokes to the nose, leaving some areas white. I switch to a 2B and use short strokes above and below areas of the nose to create more contrast. I also use the 2B to darken the nostrils. Switching back to the HB, I create short lines in the mouth and under the nose. At this point, I realize that the pupils look too human in my sketch—a koala actually has a narrow, vertical slit for a pupil. I sharpen the HB and use it to redraw the pupils and darken them. I also use the HB to form the eyelids and brows with short, directional strokes. I use the 2B to darken the irises and areas around the eyes.

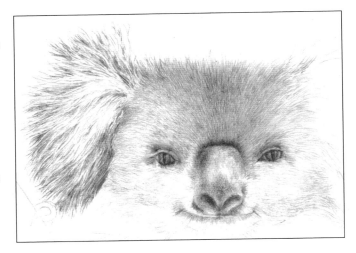

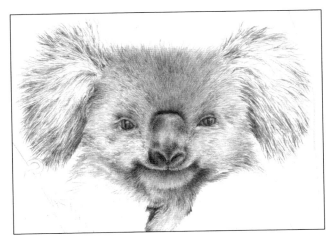

**◄ Step 6** Alternating between my sharp HB and 2B pencils, I build up the fur all over the face and chin. I use the 2B to create dark shadows around the mouth, nose, chin, and cheeks; then I use the HB like a tortillon to blend the tone. Using both pencils and circular strokes, I further develop the tone on the nose, creating a dark, leathery texture. Turning to the eyes, I define the darks with the 2B and accentuate the shape and form with the HB. I also slightly widen the eyes by darkening the lower lids. Then I carefully lift out a highlight in each eye with adhesive putty. Now I concentrate on the ear on the right, repeating steps 2 and 3. I don't finish the ear completely.

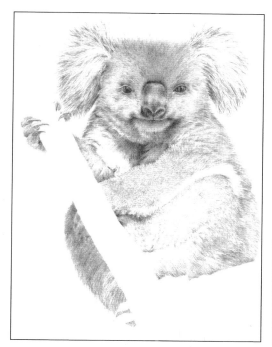

**◄ Step 7** After lightening the outline of the body with a kneaded eraser, I use short, light strokes with a 2H pencil to create the undercoat for the entire body. Again, I always draw in the direction of the fur growth and avoid creating patterns. I leave the chest and underarms white, but cover the rest of the body with a light network of interlacing 2H strokes. The fur on the arms is the shortest and most random in direction, so I make my lines reflect this. I notice that I've made the fur on the koala's leg (near the main branch) too patterned and regular; I will remedy this by adding some overlapping strokes as I darken this area in the next step. Now I add tone to both paws with the HB pencil, and I draw the long claws.

**► Step 8** I work over the entire body at once with very sharp HB and 2B pencils. I use the 2B to create the blackest areas near the white fur—the 2B "cuts" into the white areas, forming white "hairs"—I refer to my reference photo to see how the fur curls and swirls over areas of the body. I add some overlapping strokes on the left side of the body to avoid creating a pattern.

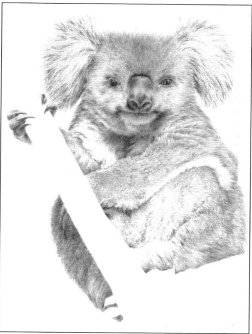

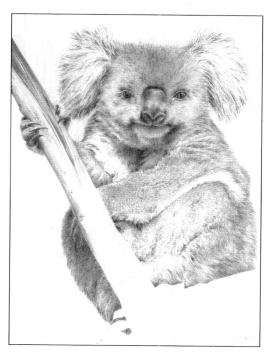

**◄ Step 9** I create a light background at the top of the image with a dull F wood-cased pencil. Then I begin adding tone to the main tree branch with 2H and HB pencils, using my entire hand and wrist to create long, smooth strokes. I build up the tone of the branch as a series of long lines of different values, creating the lined texture of a eucalyptus tree. I also add some spots and nicks with the HB to add more texture.

▶ **Step 10** Now I use an HB pencil to add the slightly curved shadows cast on the branch by the koala's fingers and claws. Then I use the 2B to deepen the tone of the shadows, as well as darken and intensify the hand and claws to create more form. I continue working down the branch, alternating between the 2H and 2B pencils. I add tone to the fattest part of the branch, where the koala rests, and create the three strips of bark hanging over this wide section. The tree branches in this drawing frame the work nicely; they also keep the viewer's eye from straying out of the picture by forming a visual "wall" that leads the eye back into the center of the work.

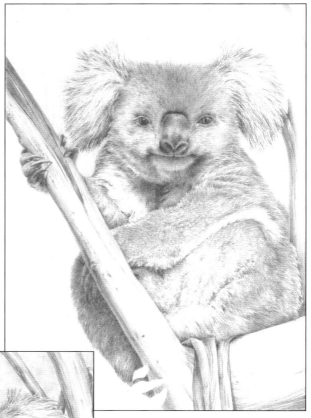

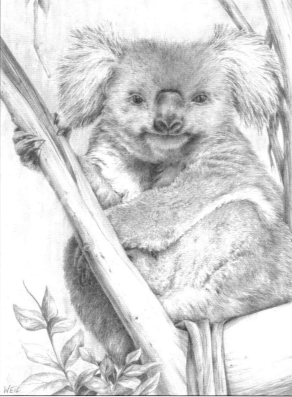

◀ **Step 11** Now that my drawing is nearly finished, I just need to complete the background and foreground leaves. I create the foreground leaves with an HB pencil and loose, soft lines. I am not too concerned with accuracy and detail here; these leaves simply add compositional balance. Now I add tone to the branches behind the koala, using the technique from step 9. I make the branches behind the ear on the right fairly dark, as this makes the white fur of the ear advance forward. Then I finish the ear by adding a bit more detail, allowing the hairs to overlap the branch. I switch to an F pencil to add more tone in the background. Instead of creating defined shapes, I use circular strokes and let my hand sort of wander about the area. I add a short, hanging branch in the upper-left corner. This branch has less contrast than the others, making it recede behind the koala and providing a sense of depth; it also adds to the framing effect and helps complete the composition.

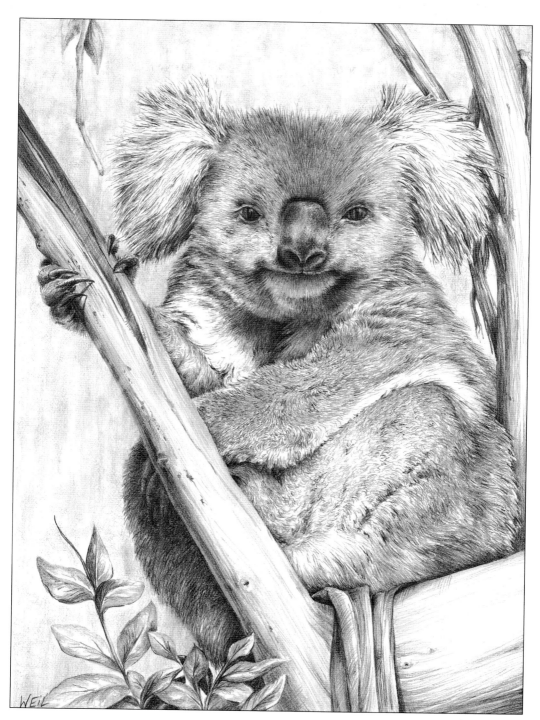

**Step 12** To finish, I add final touches with an HB pencil—I deepen some tones for more contrast, add detail lines in the eyes and nose, and build up just a bit more fur texture all over the body. I am very pleased with this drawing and the "framed" composition.

# DINGO

A portrait is a drawing of the head of a human or animal that shows the subject's face and expression. A good portrait will reveal something of the subject's character or personality. In human portraiture, the subject often is drawn from a straight-on view. This viewpoint can be exceedingly difficult when drawing animals due to the amount of foreshortening that would be required in rendering the nose, muzzle, or beak. I prefer to use a three-quarter view, where the head of the animal is turned slightly, as I find it easier to correctly portray the length and proportions of the nose from this angle. This portrait is of a dingo, which is an Australian wild dog. These beautiful animals share many features with domestic dogs, but I find that their eyes look slightly feral and untrusting. It is this wild, undomesticated look that I want to portray in my drawing.

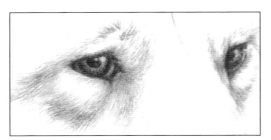

◄ **Step 1** After carefully tracing the shape of the head and the major features from my reference photo, I transfer the outline to my art paper. Then I establish the eyes (see "Drawing the Eyes" on page 43). Now I start developing the surrounding fur. I lay down light, short strokes with a sharp 2H pencil, drawing in the direction of fur growth. Then I build a layer of HB pencil on top of this lighter layer, keeping the point very sharp. Next I softly blend the 2H and HB strokes using linear strokes with an F pencil.

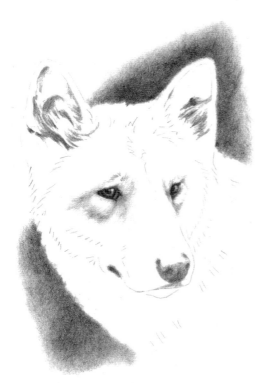

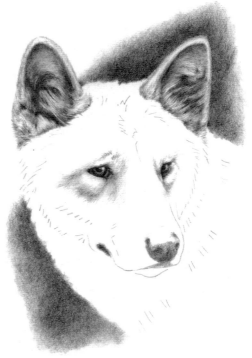

**Step 2** Using a 2B woodless pencil and circular strokes, I create the dark area behind the dingo's head (similar to the background for the tiger cub on page 33). I use the same pencil and technique for the nose and mouth, adding layers upon layers until I achieve a soft, dense black. I also use the 2B woodless pencil to lay down dark, thick linear strokes in the ears.

**Step 3** I secure a sheet of clean paper over the eyes. Then I use a sharp HB pencil to layer linear strokes over the entire ear area, varying the lengths of the strokes and leaving areas of the paper white. When finished, I use a sharp 2B to deepen these shadow areas. Then I use an F pencil and soft, circular strokes to blend the tones along the edges and within the inner "cups" of the ears.

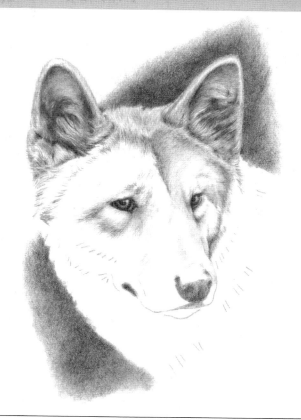

▶ **Step 4** Now I carefully move the clean sheet of paper down to protect the lower half of my drawing. Then, using a sharp 2H mechanical pencil, I apply quick, short strokes over the top of the head and around the forehead and eyes. I leave large areas of the paper white to depict the dingo's light, straw-colored fur. Next I use a well-sharpened HB mechanical pencil to layer strokes on top of the 2H undercoat, creating variations in tone and a sense of texture. Where the fur flips up around the ears and for the crease down the center of the forehead, I use a blunt F pencil to softly blend and deepen the tones.

## Drawing the Eyes

**Step 1** I start by making very light, circular strokes with a blunt H pencil over areas of the eyeball in shadow. This is done very lightly; I just want a faint base to start with.

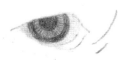

**Step 2** Now I use a sharp (but not fine-pointed) HB to create radiating lines in the iris. I use the same pencil to create the outer dark ring of the iris, as well as a solid tone that fills the pupil. I am not too worried about highlights at this stage.

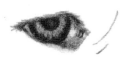

**Step 3** With a 2B pencil, I deepen the dark areas of the pupil and the ring around the iris. I use an HB pencil to deepen the tones of the whites of the eyeball with soft, circular strokes. I also use the HB to define the "eyeliner" around the eye, as well as create the round area in the corner of the eye.

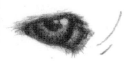

**Step 4** I use a 2B to darken the "eyeliner," pupil, and the ring around the iris. With a blunt F pencil, I add a light tone over the entire surface of the eyeball, blending the softer 2B back into the irises. Then I use the HB to go over the lines in the iris and the hair surrounding the eye. I also hint at eyelashes. I knead a bit of adhesive putty into a sharp point and lift out the highlight.

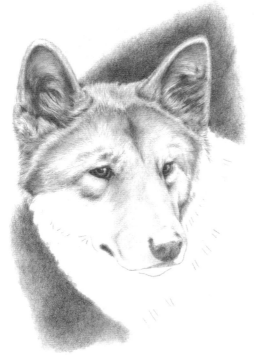

◄ **Step 5** I continue the same technique on the left side of the face. When finished, I add sharp 2B strokes around the forehead crease, eyebrows, and temple ridges for added contrast and texture. Then, using a slightly blunt F pencil, I add soft circular strokes across the forehead and down the muzzle, creating a soft tone that blends into the linework.

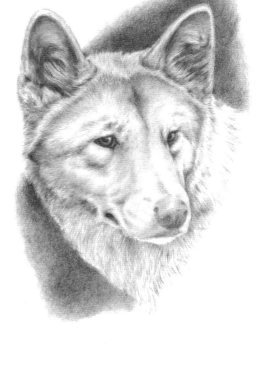

▶ **Step 6** I repeat step 5 over the bottom half of the face and on the muzzle, slowly building up the tones. Using circular strokes and an F pencil, I blend the tones over the muzzle and nose. Then I use a 2B pencil to fill in the corner of the mouth; I also create some linear strokes around the jaw. I switch to an HB and create denser, thicker, longer lines for the undercoat of the neck, adding darker strokes over the shadowed part of the neck. I leave quite a bit of white paper exposed to suggest the fur on the upper right side of the neck.

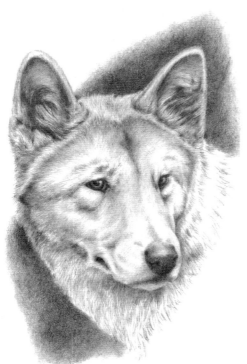

◄ **Step 7** Returning to the nose, I use a blunt 2B with a rounded tip and light, circular strokes to create the leathery surface. I am careful to leave a highlight on the tip of the nose. I lightly work this area again and again with the 2B pencil, being careful not to use too much pressure and keeping the pencil on the paper's surface at all times. Then I add one more layer of graphite to the entire nose area using an F pencil, blending the underlying 2B layers. It's better to build darks with successive layers of graphite rather than using heavy pressure, as too much pressure will create a shiny area in the tone. Switching back to the sharp 2B, I add some darker linework under the chin and on both sides of the neck. Once the 2B pencil point has dulled a little, I start to increase the depth of the tone around the lips and on the crease of the upper lip.

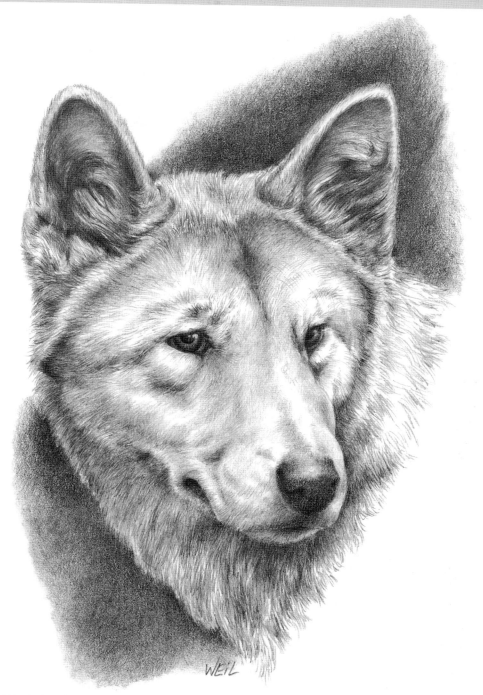

**Step 8** Using the 2H and HB pencils, I work over the face, refining and building up the texture of the fur with additional linework. I do the same with the HB and 2B on the neck and around the nose. Note how the darker fur of the neck in the lower right area defines the shape of the muzzle. Although I do not add much detail to the fur on the right side, the eye perceives the impression of fur. Now I use the 2B to add several more layers of circular strokes to the left side of the background near the neck. After sharpening the 2B, I intensify the dark edges all over the face: the corner and front of the mouth, under the mouth, the nasal openings, the "eyeliner" and pupils, the dark fur on the forehead, and the darkest fur in the ears. When you've reached the final stages of a drawing like this, it is always difficult to know where to stop. If you overwork the drawing, you'll create unsightly shiny spots, and if you add too little shading, it will appear unfinished. It helps to walk away from your work for an hour or two and return to it later with a fresh eye. After doing so, I decide that I'm happy with the dingo at this stage. He has a certain air of suspicion about him that I like, so I declare the drawing finished.

# LION PROFILE

A profile view of an animal can be very dramatic. Seeing only one side of the face can bring out the animal's distinctive features, such as a long muzzle or magnificent mane, as seen here in this profile of a lion. Because parts of the face appear more prominent in profile, be careful not to allow any one feature to dominate the drawing. Take your time working out the proportions before drawing the complete portrait.

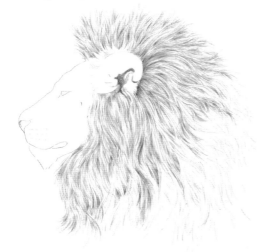

**◄ Step 1** After using the rough sketch from page 19 to create the basic outline of the lion, I transfer the outline to hot-pressed paper and use a sharp 2H pencil to start the mane. Following the technique for drawing long hair (page 16), I quickly draw clumps of long strokes over the entire mane area. Then I use a sharp HB to build up a second layer of hair. I keep my strokes long and am sure to overlap clumps. The hair needs to be messy and chaotic (I don't want my lion to look like a pampered poodle), so I allow my lines to move in different directions. After creating the second layer over the top three-quarters of the head, I switch to a sharp 2B and add a few darker strokes here and there for shadows. I also fill in some of the ear.

**► Step 2** With an always-sharp HB, I work over the entire mane, building up clumps and swirls. Once I'm satisfied with the mane, I place a sheet of paper over it to protect it from smudging. Still using the sharp HB, I build up the fur around the ear with short, tight strokes. Then I use a blunt F pencil to create darker tone inside the ear, followed by even darker strokes with the 2B. I add more strokes on top of this with the 2H. Now I remove the paper and return to the mane, developing more contrast by deepening the shadows between the individual hairs (the white of the paper) with a 2B pencil. Next I use a blunt F pencil to lightly fill in areas between clumps, again creating darker areas of shadow. These darker areas help make the white and light areas advance, giving depth to the mane.

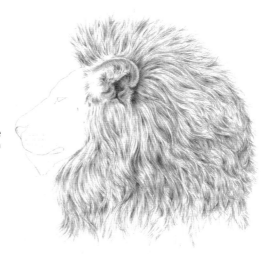

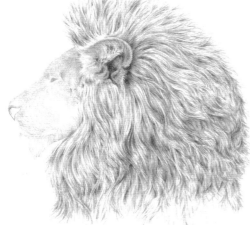

**◄ Step 3** I repeat the technique from step 2 over the entire mane and ear, increasing the contrast and depth. After covering the mane with a sheet of paper and lightening the outline of the face with a kneaded eraser, I use a sharp HB to draw very short strokes all over the face. For darker areas, I draw the strokes very close to one another; for lighter areas, I draw them farther apart. The hairs on the temple and around the ears cross one another and fall across the face in different directions for a messy look. The longer hair of the "beard" is lighter than elsewhere on the face, so I leave white areas of paper showing through. Now I softly fill in the eye with a blunt F pencil.

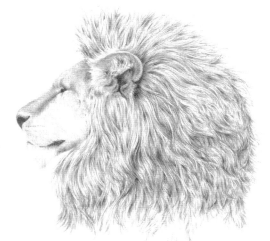

**◄ Step 4** Using the 2B pencil, I create a flat tone on the nose and around the corner of the mouth. To create lighter areas in the mouth, I lift out tone with a bit of flattened adhesive putty, holding the putty so the edge follows the direction of the hair. I use a sharp HB to layer short strokes all over the face, using the same technique as in step 3. This builds up different depths of tone on the face, helping form the structure. I use the crosshatching technique to form the brow and the corner of the eye. With a very light touch and a 2B pencil, I add the whisker dots. Whiskers are as individual as fingerprints and are used by field biologists to identify lions.

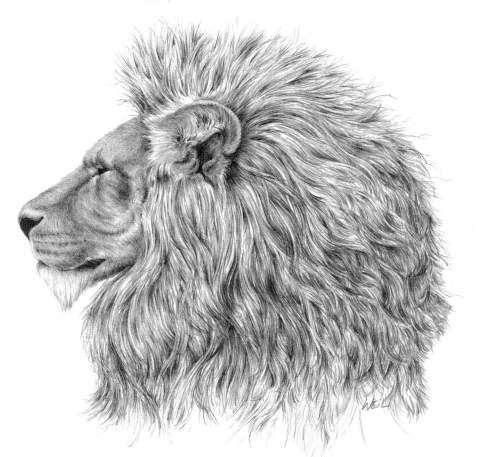

**Step 5** I continue to use the sharp HB pencil to stroke lightly over the face, building up more layers of fine fur. I also crosshatch over the cheek to enhance its tone and texture. I use a 2B to darken the inner edge of the eye and the tip of the nose, as well as add some details to the whisker markings. Still using the 2B, I create some darker lines around the eyes, on the cheek and forehead, under the jaw, and in the "beard." I also carefully shade underneath the top lip to enhance the light fur of the "beard." Now I remove the protective paper and work over the entire drawing with sharp 2B and HB pencils, adding dark values and details around and inside the ear and in select areas of the mane. Finally, with a very sharp HB, I add a few crinkly hairs around the edge of the mane to create a less-sculpted edge. Looking at this completed profile drawing, I am pleased with the result. The lion's classic pose and full mane make him look very proud.

# KANGAROO

Australia's iconic marsupial is an ideal subject to photograph, as it often is found in a stationary pose, either grazing or watching. This kangaroo, with its head gazing directly at the viewer and its large tail resting on the ground, is a good example of the quiet nature of these graceful animals.

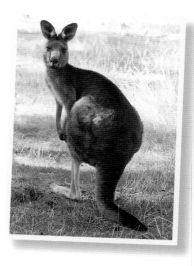

▶ **Experimenting with Texture** A kangaroo's coat is thick and dense, with an even color and texture. I always enjoy exploring the swirls and flow of the fur texture in my kangaroo drawings.

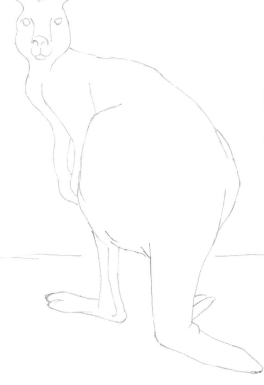

◀ **Step 1** Using an enlarged photocopy of the reference photo, I trace the outline of the kangaroo on a piece of sketch paper. I also trace the eyes, muzzle, nose, mouth, a few small fur details, and the horizon line, which I'll use later to "ground" the animal with grass. Then, using a 2 mm clutch pencil with an HB lead, I transfer my sketch to a sheet of hot-pressed paper.

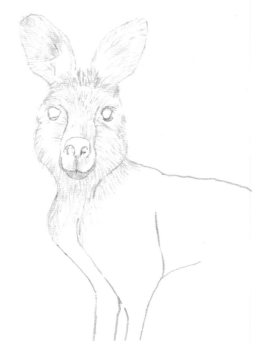

▶ **Step 2** I carefully lighten the outline of the head by dabbing at it with a kneaded eraser, leaving only a faint guideline. Starting with the ears and working down the head, I use a sharp 2H clutch lead to draw quick, short strokes for the undercoat, which will act as a directional guide for the rest of the fur. I leave the eyes and highlights of the cheeks, muzzle, and ears white.

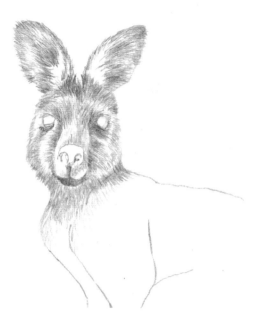

◀ **Step 3** With a well-sharpened HB clutch lead, I begin to build up the second layer of fur. Still using swift, short strokes and following the direction of fur growth, I concentrate on building deeper tones and form. Sharpening my pencil often, I keep the stroke length and starting points fairly random to avoid unattractive edges or ridges. I take care to avoid the white highlight areas.

▶ **Step 4** With a slightly blunt HB clutch lead, I use a circular motion to build up a dark, even tone for the eyes and leathery nose. I gradually build up layers of tone as I draw over these areas again and again, taking care to not press too hard. To create the highlight in each eye, I form a kneaded eraser to a point and lift out some tone. With a very sharp 2B clutch lead, I delicately accentuate the edges of the eyes and nostrils, deepening the darkest areas.

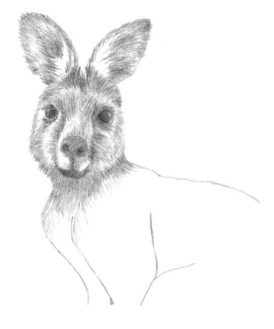

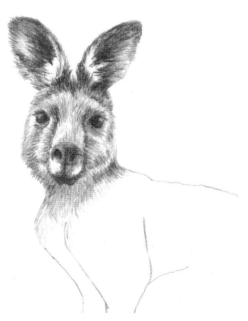

◀ **Step 5** Still using the 2B lead and sharpening it often, I build up the darkest areas of the fur on the head with short strokes. I always follow the direction of the fur as I work, deepening the tone to create contrast across the nose, mouth, and ears. I pay particular attention to creating dark tones in the ears, as these areas provide the negative space that creates the white areas (see page 10). The deep tone in the inner ear helps create the appearance of white fur tufts on the outer ear. I carefully add a few 2B strokes into this white area to create an even greater sense of depth and make the white fur stand out.

▶ **Step 6** I go over the entire head area once again with fine strokes of a sharp HB clutch lead, further refining the details. This final layer helps blend the underlying layers and creates an even, smooth texture. Next I continue the linework down the neck, alternating HB and 2H leads. This blends the finished area of the head into the body. I use the same techniques that I used for the head as I continue down the body. First I carefully lighten the outline with my kneaded eraser. Then, with a sharp 2H clutch lead, I work down the forearms and the back of the kangaroo, following the direction of the fur and trying not to create any obvious patterns or edges when I apply my strokes. I refer to my reference photo often to make sure I am following the fur direction correctly.

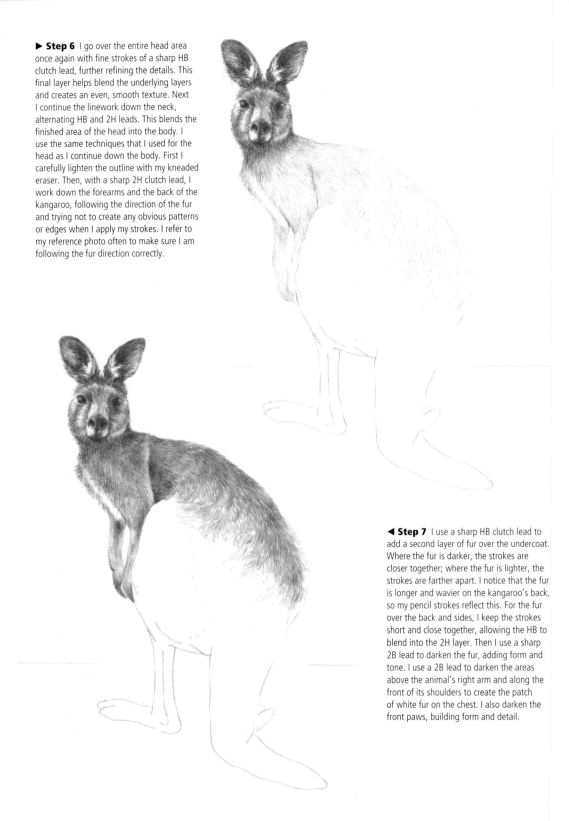

◀ **Step 7** I use a sharp HB clutch lead to add a second layer of fur over the undercoat. Where the fur is darker, the strokes are closer together; where the fur is lighter, the strokes are farther apart. I notice that the fur is longer and wavier on the kangaroo's back, so my pencil strokes reflect this. For the fur over the back and sides, I keep the strokes short and close together, allowing the HB to blend into the 2H layer. Then I use a sharp 2B lead to darken the fur, adding form and tone. I use a 2B lead to darken the areas above the animal's right arm and along the front of its shoulders to create the patch of white fur on the chest. I also darken the front paws, building form and detail.

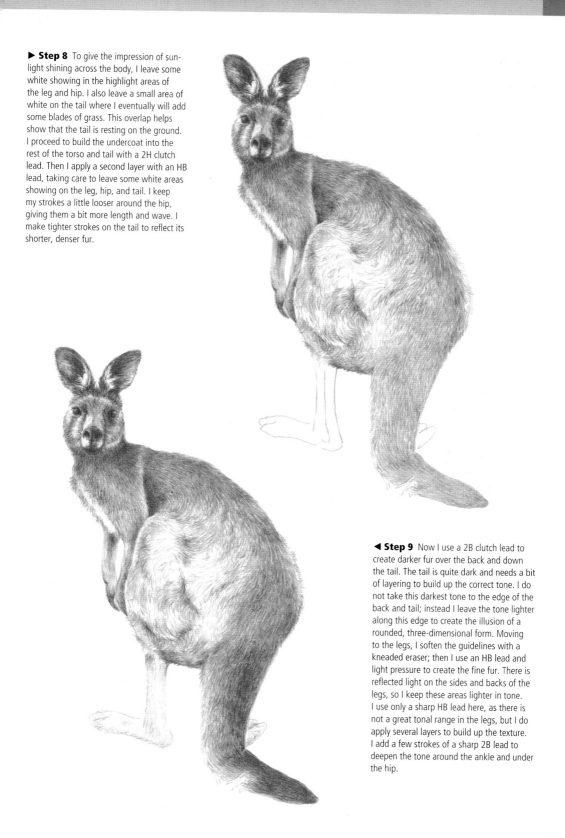

▶ **Step 8** To give the impression of sunlight shining across the body, I leave some white showing in the highlight areas of the leg and hip. I also leave a small area of white on the tail where I eventually will add some blades of grass. This overlap helps show that the tail is resting on the ground. I proceed to build the undercoat into the rest of the torso and tail with a 2H clutch lead. Then I apply a second layer with an HB lead, taking care to leave some white areas showing on the leg, hip, and tail. I keep my strokes a little looser around the hip, giving them a bit more length and wave. I make tighter strokes on the tail to reflect its shorter, denser fur.

◀ **Step 9** Now I use a 2B clutch lead to create darker fur over the back and down the tail. The tail is quite dark and needs a bit of layering to build up the correct tone. I do not take this darkest tone to the edge of the back and tail; instead I leave the tone lighter along this edge to create the illusion of a rounded, three-dimensional form. Moving to the legs, I soften the guidelines with a kneaded eraser; then I use an HB lead and light pressure to create the fine fur. There is reflected light on the sides and backs of the legs, so I keep these areas lighter in tone. I use only a sharp HB lead here, as there is not a great tonal range in the legs, but I do apply several layers to build up the texture. I add a few strokes of a sharp 2B lead to deepen the tone around the ankle and under the hip.

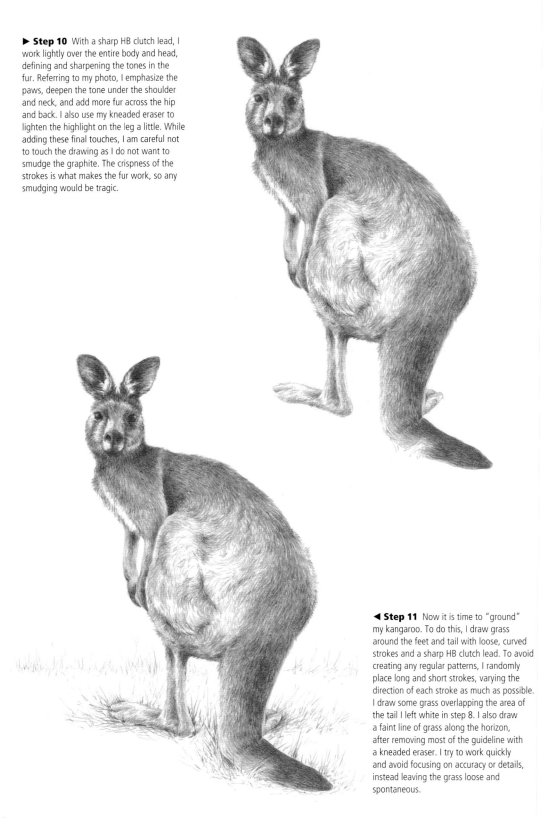

▶ **Step 10** With a sharp HB clutch lead, I work lightly over the entire body and head, defining and sharpening the tones in the fur. Referring to my photo, I emphasize the paws, deepen the tone under the shoulder and neck, and add more fur across the hip and back. I also use my kneaded eraser to lighten the highlight on the leg a little. While adding these final touches, I am careful not to touch the drawing as I do not want to smudge the graphite. The crispness of the strokes is what makes the fur work, so any smudging would be tragic.

◀ **Step 11** Now it is time to "ground" my kangaroo. To do this, I draw grass around the feet and tail with loose, curved strokes and a sharp HB clutch lead. To avoid creating any regular patterns, I randomly place long and short strokes, varying the direction of each stroke as much as possible. I draw some grass overlapping the area of the tail I left white in step 8. I also draw a faint line of grass along the horizon, after removing most of the guideline with a kneaded eraser. I try to work quickly and avoid focusing on accuracy or details, instead leaving the grass loose and spontaneous.

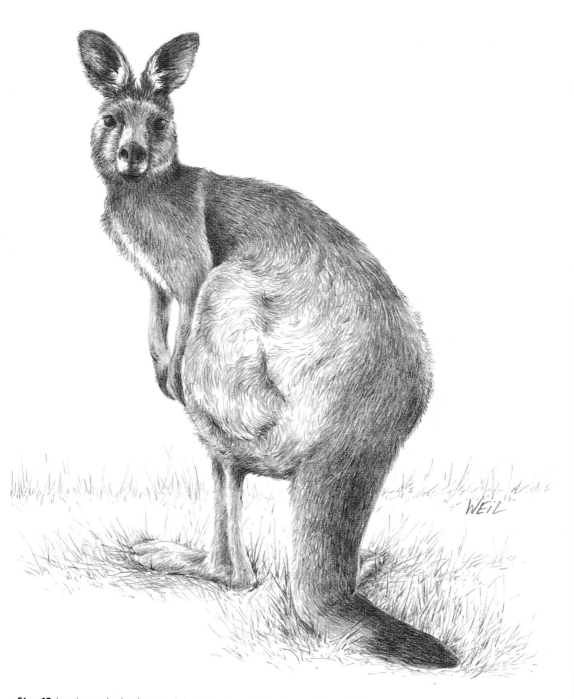

**Step 12** I continue to develop the grass, darkening the tone under the kangaroo's feet to further ground the animal. When I'm satisfied with my drawing, I sign the work and lightly spray the entire drawing with workable fixative to help prevent smudging.

# GIRAFFES IN A LANDSCAPE

Many of my animal drawings are portraits with little or no surrounding backgrounds. But sometimes I want to show more of the relationship between an animal and its environment, so I'll place the animal in a larger landscape. There are several important aspects to carefully consider when creating this type of composition:

1. How and where is the animal placed in its environment?
2. How do dominant features such as large trees, rocks, and mountains affect the size and placement of the animal and its visibility?
3. How do the animal(s) and other dominant features affect the balance of the composition?
4. Does the vegetation directly relate to the animal? Does it match the animal's natural habitat?
5. Is there a distinct foreground, middle ground, and background?

For this study, I chose to draw a group of giraffes in a savannah of South Africa. I wanted my landscape to emphasize the vastness of the savannah, the extreme height of the giraffes, and the glowing heat of the midday sun.

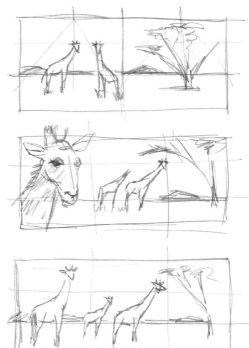

▶ **Thumbnail Sketches** To work out the composition, I start by drawing several thumbnail sketches. I create these small sketches quickly, showing only the basic elements of the drawing. My first attempt seems too static and staged, and the composition is too symmetrical. I like the second thumbnail better, but the large giraffe head detracts from the rest of the landscape. The third sketch is the most pleasing—the page is divided into thirds horizontally and vertically, and the broad sky produces a sense of vastness.

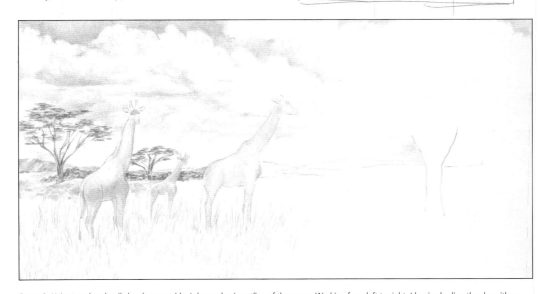

**Step 1** Using my thumbnail sketch as a guide, I draw a basic outline of the scene. Working from left to right, I begin shading the sky with a light layer of F pencil. I leave many areas white to represent the clouds, lightly shading their undersides with an HB to suggest form. I create the trees in the background with both 2B and HB pencils using crosshatching and scrumbling techniques. Then I begin to build up tone on the giraffes with an F pencil. I also use a 2H pencil to lightly create the grass in the foreground, using short, randomly placed strokes.

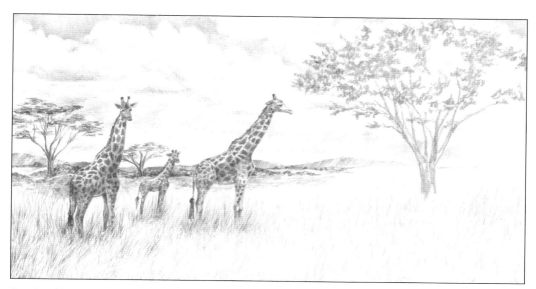

**Step 2** I add more grass and detail to the left side of the background. Then I create the spots and details on the giraffe at left with a sharp 2B pencil and do the same on the young middle giraffe but with a sharp HB pencil. I add detail to the giraffe at right with a 2B and then use F, HB, and 2B pencils to slowly add tone to the distant bushes and mountains. I keep the detail very minimal in these distant areas. When drawing landscapes, keep in mind that objects closest to you will be sharper and have a greater amount of detail. As objects recede, they have less contrast and become more indistinct. (You can see how I've employed this phenomenon—called "atmospheric perspective"—by looking at the final drawing; notice how the sharp detail in the foreground tree brings it forward.) Now I work on the foreground tree. I start with a 2H and roughly draw across an area, then work over it in stages with an HB and a 2B. When drawing trees, try drawing "clumps" of leaf shapes, rather than trying to draw each individual leaf. Approach trees in stages, building up more and more "clumps" of tone to represent the leaves. This also applies when drawing large areas of grass.

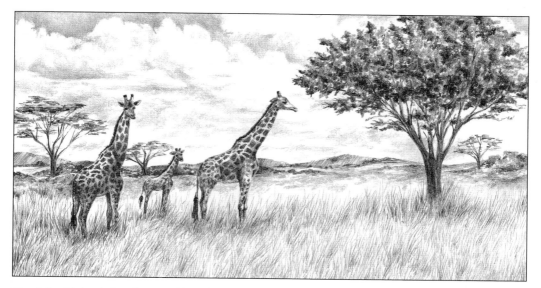

**Step 3** Now I darken the fur, tails, ears, and faces of the giraffes with the 2B to bring them forward as focal points of the drawing. I add more grass to the foreground, loosely drawing long and short strokes. (I use the HB pencil for lighter areas and the 2B for darker ones.) I leave a band of white paper between the top of the grass and the background elements, as this helps create a sense of distance and the appearance of a slight haze from the heat. I add a few more leaf clumps to the left-hand tree, creating a leaf canopy for the giraffes to take shelter under. Finally, I create the right-hand side of the background, making these elements the smallest and most distant. Although this drawing is small, it produces a sense of depth and space. It also succeeds in creating a natural environment for the animals.

# ZEBRA IN MOTION

Animals are always moving! Photos can capture animals "frozen" in action; referring to them while drawing is easier than trying to capture movement in progress. You can depict an animal's action by adding a few clues in your drawing. For example, one or two feet may be off the ground, the head may be erect, the tail may appear to sway, the ears and eyes may appear alert, and there may be visible muscle tension in the moving limbs. You also may use other clues relative to the surrounding landscape: the grass may be bent and the animal's feet may kick up dust. You also can use staggered movement lines and blurred edges to enhance the feeling of motion.

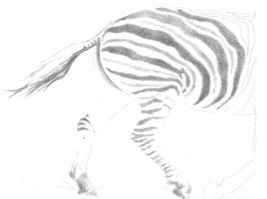

◀ **Step 1** After transferring an outline of the zebra to drawing paper, I use a sharp 2B pencil to create an even, dark tone on the thick stripes over the back of the animal. I add two or three layers to darken the tone where the animal is rounded out and in shadow. I also draw the thinner stripes with a 2B, but I do not layer them as heavily. I add dark tone between the haunches and loose, flowing dark lines along the tail. The tone on the lower leg stripes is not as sharp as it is along the haunches because the lower leg stripes will be blurred later in the drawing. With the stripes in place, I create muscle tension by lifting some areas of graphite with a kneaded eraser.

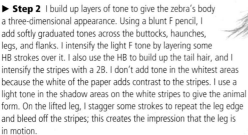

▶ **Step 2** I build up layers of tone to give the zebra's body a three-dimensional appearance. Using a blunt F pencil, I add softly graduated tones across the buttocks, haunches, legs, and flanks. I intensify the light F tone by layering some HB strokes over it. I also use the HB to build up the tail hair, and I intensify the stripes with a 2B. I don't add tone in the whitest areas because the white of the paper adds contrast to the stripes. I use a light tone in the shadow areas on the white stripes to give the animal form. On the lifted leg, I stagger some strokes to repeat the leg edge and bleed off the stripes; this creates the impression that the leg is in motion.

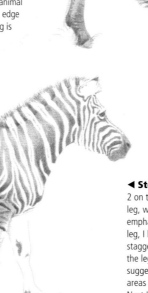

◀ **Step 3** I repeat the technique from step 2 on the face and the zebra's right front leg, working with F, HB, and 2B pencils. To emphasize rapid movement on the lifted leg, I keep the edges soft and draw several staggered strokes along the forward edge of the leg. I shade the hoof very loosely, which suggests motion. I then begin lightly shading areas of the zebra's front right leg and hoof. Next I sharpen the 2B and use short, swift strokes for the stiff hairs of the mane.

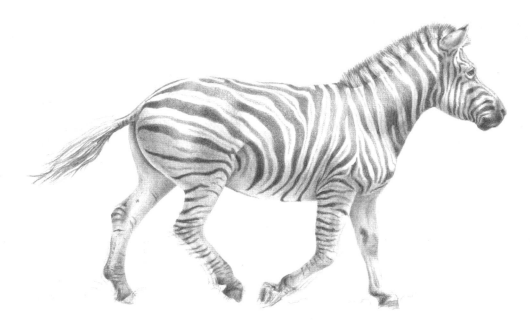

**Step 4** With a very sharp HB pencil, I carefully add shadowed areas to the mane (even in the darker 2B areas), allowing plenty of white paper to show through for the white stripes. Then I work some tone into the zebra's left front leg with F and HB pencils. This leg has very little striping but is darker in tone than the upper body, as it is in shadow. The leg also is firmly planted as the zebra steps forward, so I do not draw any movement lines or blurred edges. I create the darker spot and hock with a 2B. Now, with my F and HB pencils, I concentrate on rendering the tones that create the three-dimensional qualities of the neck and face. Again I let the white of the paper show through with lightly contrasting tone in the shadow areas to create form. I intensify the deepest blacks of the shadowed stripes, the eye, and the nostril with a 2B. The body of the zebra is now complete.

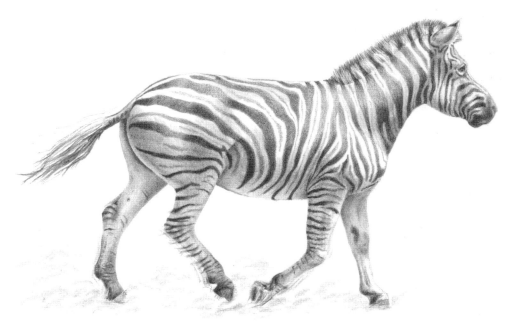

**Step 5** Now I add some billowing dust under and behind the zebra's feet to suggest that she is kicking up dust as she moves. To do this, I use a blunt F pencil to lightly draw soft scrumble lines around the feet and behind the zebra.

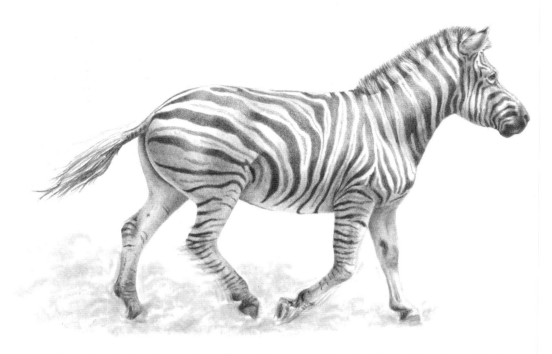

**Step 6** I blur and blend the F tone from step 5 into swirling, puffy shapes. I also lightly and carefully blur the lower legs, softening the edges into the raised dust. If you don't have a tortillon, try using a cotton swab.

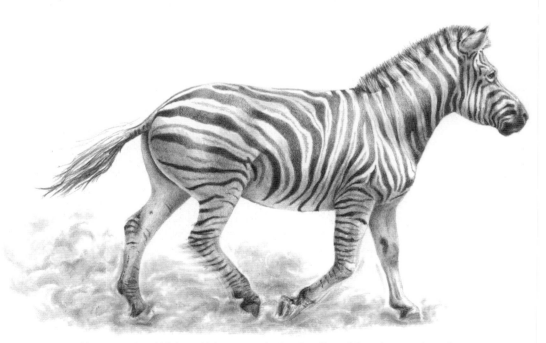

**Step 7** I use a blunt HB pencil to add darker and lighter tones to the dust; then I blur and shape them using the tortillon. By now my tortillon has picked up a bit of graphite on its tip, so I use this to "draw" with as well. I use circular and curving motions with my tortillon to blend the graphite into swirling dust shapes.

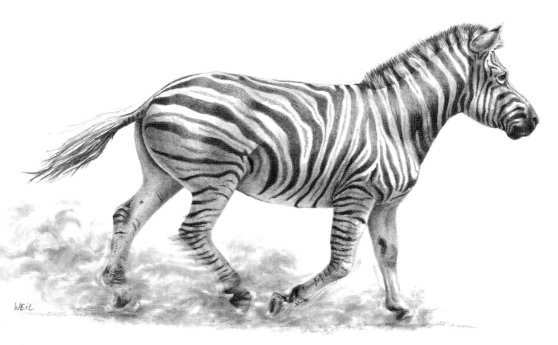

WEIL

**Step 8** In step 6, the feet and legs are distinct; here you can see that the legs and hooves merge into the billowing dust. I mold a piece of adhesive putty into a rough cylinder shape and gently drag it across the feet, legs, and dust. This lifts off some of the graphite in the darker foot/leg area to match the tones of the dust. I use the tortillon to blur the dust back over the legs and feet and to further soften the edges of the lower legs. Dragging the tortillon across the darker stripes, I pull some graphite into the swirling dust; then I use the residue of the graphite on the tortillon to drag some tone back over the legs and puff up more dust around the hooves. (Practice this on a sheet of paper before trying this on your final work.) With an HB pencil, I scribble in the impression of small pebbles under the hooves. Finally, I use the HB and 2B pencils to intensify the stripes, shadows, and dust. Now my zebra is complete.

## Depicting Animals in Motion

*There are a few tricks to representing motion. Note how the pose and body language conveys action. The zebra at bottom left is at a slow walk. The head is lowered, three of the feet are on the ground, the tail is flicking back and forth, and the forward foot is slightly lifted. Everything about this pose suggests languid, relaxed motion.*

*The zebra at bottom center is just breaking out into a trot. The head is lifted, the ears and eyes are forward, and the tail is raised. Two of the feet are lifted off the ground, the third rear foot is just about to kick back, and the leading foot has stepped forward. This pose suggests brisk motion.*

*The zebra at bottom right is in a gallop. The head is up and thrown slightly back. The ears are back, the nostrils are open, and the tail is streaming behind. The back is arched and the feet are off the ground.*

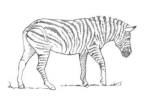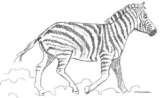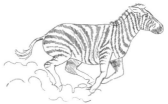

# GROUP OF MEERKATS

One of the most interesting things about drawing animals is exploring the way they interact with one another. The original photo references for this composition (on page 23) show a group of meerkats huddled together for warmth. The location of each animal is a direct result of their social standing in the group, and the warmest meerkat of all is the one at the bottom with a very smug look on its face. All the others are huddled around and on top of it, each trying to squirm its way into a warmer spot.

As well as showing animal interaction, this drawing also explores the use of dark areas of negative space to determine and enhance the overall tonal range of a work. In the photos on page 23, you'll see that the background, eyes, and noses are very dark, and the meerkats' coats are very light. Meerkats actually are a medium to light brown, but the black background makes them appear lighter than they actually are. I need to be careful not to be fooled into making them too light.

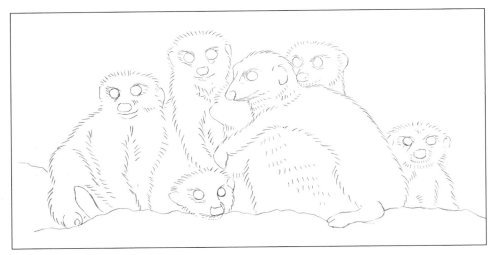

**Step 1** I use a high-resolution print of my final reference photo to trace the outlines of the meerkats, and I transfer this onto my drawing paper. Keep in mind that the outline sketch is just a guide—don't be afraid to change things if you feel the photo has distorted the image in some way. Instead of using a solid outline, which is more restricting, I use short strokes to create furry edges for the meerkats. I will lighten these lines as I work, but I won't completely erase them—I'll incorporate them later when I start drawing the actual fur.

▶ **Step 2** I establish the darkest areas first so I can judge how to build up the contrast between the background and the meerkats as I work. Using a sharp 2B pencil and layers of circular strokes, I add the eyes, ears, and noses, trying to leave a highlight in each eye. Then I use a very sharp HB to add details, such as the pupils, rims around the eyes, and nostrils. When these areas are as dark as I want them, I mold a piece of adhesive putty to a point and carefully dab at the eyes to lift out highlights. I also do this around the eye markings to soften the edges.

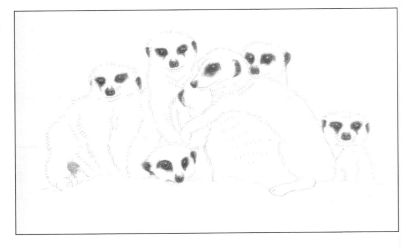

► **Step 3** It is necessary to start establishing the dark background early in this work; otherwise the meerkats could become too dark too soon. Here I start filling in the background using a woodless 2B pencil that has a blunt, flattened edge. I use soft, small, circular motions to build up areas of tone, making sure my pencil doesn't leave the paper. I work from right to left, slowly filling the entire background with a mottled tone. I also turn the drawing around as I draw so I can work from different angles.

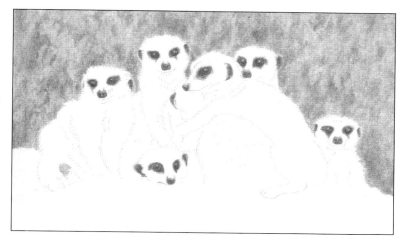

► **Step 4** I turn the drawing upright and protect the background with paper. Now I start to work up the fur on the meerkats, one animal at a time. I create the undercoats with a sharp 2H pencil, leaving white showing where the fur is lightest. I don't erase any of the outlines but allow them to become part of the overall fur by lightening them. When finished, I begin to refine the fur on the heads and around the noses and mouths with a sharp HB. Then I remove the paper and add darker tones to the background with the 2B woodless pencil.

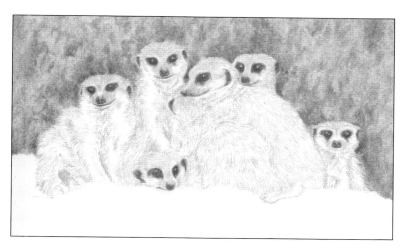

► **Step 5** I protect the right side of the drawing and use a sharp HB and short strokes on the far-left meerkat. I use a 2H for lighter areas of fur and a blunt F pencil to blend the fur in the creases and shadow areas. Returning to the background, I add a layer of circular strokes with an 8B woodless pencil. My pencil never leaves the page as it wanders around the area. I work around the edges of the meerkats, allowing the lighter hairs to define their outlines. Now I use a tortillon and tight, circular motions to soften the grainy texture of the 8B.

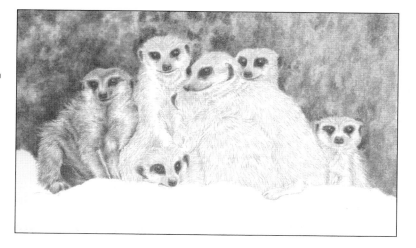

▶ **Step 6** Using the same method as in step 5, I develop the next two meerkats. Then I use a sharp HB to create the back of the head of the meerkat with her back turned. To create the coarse stripes on this meerkat (and the one hugging her), I draw the darker fur with a sharp 2B. This will create a dark tone while retaining some of the white of the paper between the strokes, giving the impression of thicker, stiffer hairs.

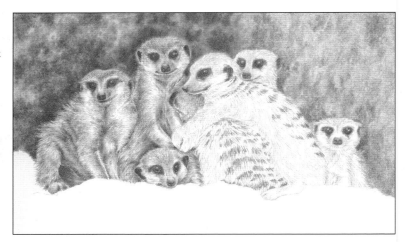

▶ **Step 7** Once the darkest areas of the stripes have been established, I can go over the entire back of the meerkat with a sharp HB pencil to create the surrounding fur. I am careful to allow the white of the paper to show through in places, giving the impression of lighter hairs. I am careful not to create any unnatural ridges or patterns, slightly varying the length and the direction of the strokes.

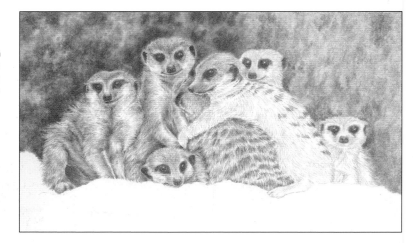

▶ **Step 8** I repeat the techniques from step 7 on the curved back of the next meerkat. I continue using the HB to add tone to the foot, building up layers where the fur is darkest. Then I repeat steps 4 and 5 to develop the face of the meerkat in the back. Next I return to the 8B and tortillon and continue adding dark values to the background. At this point, I notice that the second meerkat from the left has a strange smile (see step 7), so I use adhesive putty to remove some of the dark, upward-curving edges of the mouth.

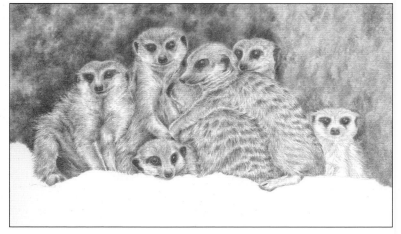

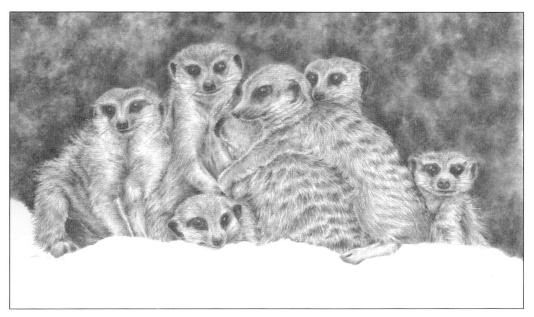

**Step 9** Using the same techniques, I complete the meerkat to the far right and then darken the right side of the background. Now I spend some time refining the drawing. Using a sharp 2H, I add more fur to the animals, especially on their faces. I use the same pencil to add more overlapping fur where the animals meet. This helps create a feeling of closeness among the animals. I also use the blunt F pencil to increase the tones in the fur creases and shadow areas. (This is most obvious when you compare the far-right meerkat above with how he appears in step 8.) Using the 8B and the tortillon, I darken the entire background, visually advancing the meerkats. Then I use a very sharp 2B to add darker details to the eyes and nostrils, as well as the very dark whiskers. Next I pull out more highlights in the eyes with the adhesive putty.

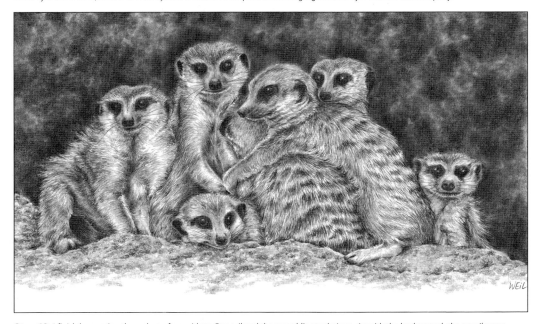

**Step 10** I finish by creating the rocky surface with an F pencil and the scrumbling technique. As with the background, the pencil never leaves the page, but the motion is looser and freer, creating a rough texture. I work very quickly and randomly across the ground area. To add shadows to the rocks, I use a blunt 2B pencil and the scrumbling technique. I usually don't use spray fixative on my work, as it can darken the overall tone of the drawing, but, in this case, it's important to fix the work as the soft 8B smudges so easily. Luckily the slight darkening of tone doesn't negatively affect this drawing.

# CLOSING WORDS

I hope you have enjoyed this book and "watching" me as I draw! I certainly had a lot of fun creating these drawings and describing how I achieved each effect. It also has been very enjoyable observing the subjects for this book. You will discover that half the pleasure of drawing animals is watching them.

You don't need a fancy studio and expensive equipment to succeed at drawing—you just need to persevere. Remember that the key to drawing well is to practice as often as you can. Experiment with different techniques, methods, and equipment to find your personal style. Try to draw something every day—you will be pleasantly surprised by how rapidly you improve. But most of all, enjoy the journey and have fun along the way.

—*Linda Weil*

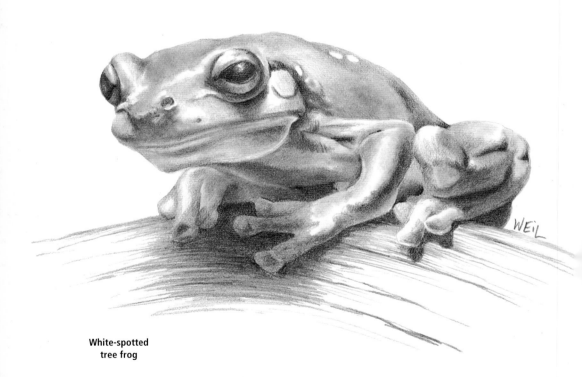

**White-spotted
tree frog**